SELF-DESTRUCTION

SELF-DESTRUCTION

✦

My Country My People

Why cant we all just get along?

Peter Brownlowe

iUniverse, Inc.

New York Lincoln Shanghai

SELF-DESTRUCTION
My Country My People

iUniverse books may be ordered through booksellers or by contacting:

iUniverse
2021 Pine Lake Road, Suite 100
Lincoln, NE 68512
www.iuniverse.com
1-800-Authors (1-800-288-4677)

ISBN-13: 978-0-595-37545-5 (pbk)
ISBN-13: 978-0-595-81939-3 (ebk)
ISBN-10: 0-595-37545-6 (pbk)
ISBN-10: 0-595-81939-7 (ebk)

Printed in the United States of America

Contents

Introduction

I am going to take you on a journey from my childhood years to adulthood. I will cover many different topics that I feel are, or should be important to the American people. I will tell my story from an African American male perspective as it relates to my people and my country. I will not stick to any one subject or topic, or have felt the need to go into details or do any extensive research on any one topic or subject. I believe many of my readers are already familiar with many of the subjects and topics that I talk about and are capable of accepting or dismissing any of my many ideas, thoughts or theories that are in my writings. This book is simply to try to make us open our eyes and think, and if any of the things that I write about are true, then we should ask ourselves should we be trying to do something about it.

I was not force or influence by anyone in any way to write this book. I believe in time everyone at some point in their lives will and should step back and take a look at what is really important in life and realize that there is noting more important on this earth than life itself. We must allow those of us who are fortunate enough to have life to live it, and be free in doing so, as long as what they're doing is not at the expense of others.

I have had the rare opportunity to witness and experience life and many of its social and economic impacts throughout my career. I will take you on a journey from the violent streets of the ghettos to the corporate ballrooms, to war in Iraq, and back to the streets.

Many of the topics in this book are subjective, opinionated and may be considered controversial. This book is not intended to single out any one person or group but it may contain many of the things that we see in individuals and groups that we consider controversial. It crosses all racial and political boundaries in order to bring attention to some of the many issues that I think we are and should be concerned about but are too scared to say or do anything about.

While reading this book, we should always keep in mind that despite what may appear as being related to a particular group or group of people, we must remember that everyone of us are individuals and should be treated as such.

I am not trying to portray myself as an expert in any one area or field because I'm not. I'm simply voicing my opinions on different subjects, topics and issues that I think is important for my people and my country. My intentions are to generate some thoughts and ideas that will make us think and possibly take a look at what we can or cannot do to help expose and fix any of theses issues if in fact he or she believes there is one that we should be concerned with.

I will do so simply by using many of my personal past and current experiences that I have witnessed and gone through that have naturally brought many of these topics close to home. I believe it will do the same for many of my readers as well. Some of us will be more familiar in certain areas than others and will be impacted differently. This book is rear and unedited and was written in a language level that is consistent and appropriate throughout for all to read and understand.

Never since Jimmy the Greek 's statement on race relation has there been a book about our people this edgy or controversial. Some of us naturally will be offended while reading this book which is a good thing, others will be delighted which is also a good thing.

This book says what everyone would like to say but are scared to say. I would treat it as a collector's item. If anyone is offended after reading this book, I do apologize in advance, however I must continue to tell my story. Our ability to express ourselves and challenge others is always a healthy thing. So without further delay I will begin to take you on my life's journey.

In The Beginning

As I was growing up as a kid in my 3rd grade elementary school, I remember sitting in my classroom and looking out my classroom widow. There I saw a police officer that would routinely patrol around the school on a daily basis.

Everyday I would watch him from my 3rd floor classroom window as he walked by swinging his baton as if he didn't have a trouble in the world. I said to myself that was what I wanted to be when I grew up. I remember thinking, wow, he does s not have to be in school like I was, he was able to go where he wanted and do what he wanted, not actually realizing that he too was being watched or what it would take to get there.

It would take me another twenty more years of life experiences to eventually get me back to where I really wanted to be and do in life. I am still not sure exactly as to what should I give the most credit to for steering me down the path to the job that I do and love so much in a country and city that I admire.

Is it the fact that I have always admired police officers and what he or she does to try and help people or is it because of life experiences that I have seen and experienced growing up in what was a cruel and violent environment? If I had to guess, I would say that it is a little bit of both.

What I do know for sure is that growing up in one of the one of the toughest housing projects in the Bronx is that obeying the laws and being patriotic was not one of the things that many of the young adults in my neighborhood were concerned about.

Through my past journeys and experiences, I have gone full circle to the point where I have become a dedicated law enforcement officer and a staunch patriot.

The Birth of the Hip-Hop Culture (The New Generation)

I will begin by taking you on a journey from the street of the ghettos as one of the pioneers of a music culture now known as rap or hip-hop. We have taken what was once known as a simple form of entertainment to another level. This form of entertainment has taken a turn to become one of the most violent cultures and genre of music that is taking our young people down the wrong path.

I am very concerned because we now have a new generation of young Americans youths that are coming up that appears to be on a path to self-destruction. One of these sectors in particular that I am concerned with is within the entertainment sector, which began, in the African American communities.

We now have a culture that has taken it to a level where entertainment and reality are now intertwined. Twisted in reference to portraying a negative act or character, and transforming it into one that is viewed in their eyes as positive, aspired and praised upon. These associations of characters and acts are intertwined in a culture that has moved in the wrong direction.

I will take you back to the beginning for a moment in time in order that we can better understand why this type of music is tainted with violence.

I can honestly speak on this subject because I was one of its original pioneers. I was there where and when it all started as a disc jockey or (DJ) back in the days in a place they called the "Boogie-down Bronx" (Bronx, New York).

Unfortunately there has always been a competitive edge to human nature that requires us to want to challenge others and to prove our superiority, no matter how silly it may be at times. A new culture was being borne out of the projects that allowed many of us to do so. We could now release some of our frustrations, become popular and even possibly become wealthy. This new culture began with break dancing and later transformed into Hip-Hop or Rap, as we now know it today.

Break dancing was a form of entertainment that we used as a form of entertainment and a tool to challenge our opponent or opponents in the form of a dance instead of fighting. We would walk in a gang-like style as they do now, sometimes in-groups and bunches to take on our opponents by challenging them to a break dancing contest. The winner would be the ones that had the best dance moves and the losers we would say were the ones who have gotten burnt or have loss the fight when it was all over.

With this came the need for more break dancing music. The preferred music called for a continued drumbeat that was long enough to allow the break-dancers to do all of their moves before the audible portions of the record would come in. There were very few albums or recordings at that time that were produced and available that had the type of long drawn out drumbeat that was required.

This leads to the need for Disc Jockeys or DJs as we referred to them back then. The DJs would mix the short drumbeats from each of the records together using two turntables and their headphones to ensure that the beats were mixed in on key. They would go shopping or beat hunting as we use to call it back then, where they would have to search high and low until they could find a beat that could be danced to. They would have to buy duplicate records with the same dance beat. The beat had to be long enough to allow the DJs to listen in the headphone while one of the beats are playing, go to the next turntable listen to the beat on the second turntable and mix in the same beat before the voice audible came back in. The quicker you were in picking up the needles and mixing in the beat portions of the records without missing the beat the better you were as a DJ. DJ's, as we knew it back them were not the ones that spoke on the mike. They were the ones whose sole purpose was to mix in the beats so that the audience could dance to.

Soon came the Introduction of the synthesizer that we use to call a Beat Box. It allowed musicians and DJs to be able to make their own beats and lengthen the duration for dancing and breaking without missing a beat or mixing records. The longer the duration of the beat the better. It allowed for more and more introductions, talking on the mike to the beat, and eventually rapping to the beat.

Initially the DJs were the star of the show. They were the ones that the dancers, the rappers, and the people came out to see to make the dancing and the rapping go smoothly. Then came the MCs, which stood for the Masters of Ceremony. The MCs would be the ones to introduce the DJs and make the DJs look good by talking on the microphone and later rapping on the microphone. The DJs continued to mix the beats for dancing, but began to shift more towards mixing for the MCs as rapping became more popular and the focus of attention began to shift towards the rappers.

The DJs began to take second fiddle at the concerts as the recording industry began to change by producing more compatible beats for rapping with longer beat portions while the introduction and the use of the Beat Box (Synthesizer) became more popular.

DJs status began and continued to fade very quickly, as he or she was no longer needed to be quick on the turntables anymore and the MCs became the dominant player from that point on. Being able to talk, rap and even sing longer on microphone began to take over. The DJs began to play second fiddle at every function and would never again regain the status of the lead entertainer.

This form of mixing and talking on the mike was normally practice in the Caribbean culture because of the long dubbing beats in most reggae recordings. It was very similar in some ways to rap but did not transform into rap, as we know it today.

As the beats got longer and the ability to capture an audience while talking on the mike while people are dancing, paved the way for rhyming and rapping on the mike as we know it today.

The mike became a tool of expression for those who had access to it. The ability to express oneself by talking and boasting on the mike was a very powerful tool used to gain and win superiority as compared to break dancing once was in the community. It became more of a vehicle that was used to give an individual or group an opportunity to do such things as tell their life story, talk about each other, boast about themselves, lash out at their opponents, and increase their popularity among their peers.

Just as break dancing was used to face off with your opponent, rapping on the mike quickly took its place. The raps that were being expressed were targeted to those in the immediate area and other opponents in the community similar to how break dancing was used to take on opponents.

In order for this type of music to be aired on the radio initially, it could not have had any violent overtones, as in the early rap recordings like Rappers Delight by the Sugarhill Gang and others from that era. Little by little the public became more accepting of this type of music. Once the public and the local media began accepting more of the violent overtones and radio stations continued to play it on the air, this new culture that we now know as rap and hip-hop was born.

Some of the original groups like DJ Africa Bambatta who was originally affiliated with the Black Spades; the name of a local street gang, tried to use his influence to help stop the violence by using this medium to get the young youths off of the streets. Others like, DJ Grand Theodore, Cool Herc the Sugarhill Gang,

Breakout, Grandmaster Flash, Doug E. Fresh, and the likes were among some of the original pioneers

Break dancing faded while rapping on the mike took its place. As this trend continued and the market for rap music grew stronger, more and more MCs began to enter the field. Block parties began popping up everywhere. They initially began popping up on the grounds of the housing projects; usually on the basketball courts, then to the city parks, at the school gyms, and later on the night clubs and concerts halls. As this type of music continued to air on radio stations, the market grew quickly as the potential to make money in this business began to spread among greedy promoters and the youths in the inner cities.

The market demand grew beyond expectations and the entertainers began to charge more and more money for their performances. The well-known rappers would draw large crowds to their performances and were able to maintain a large cover charge for admissions. Among some of the most favorite places to perform were those that were large enough to accommodate hundreds of people. Places like the local school gymnasiums, large auditoriums, clubs, and concert halls. The bigger the venue, the bigger was potential to make more money.

Rapping for money and the possibly of becoming the next rap star became the next big thing in town. Not only could you now say anything that you wanted, but you could also get paid for it as well. This allowed us to continue to take on our opponents and assert that same type of superiority that we all sought as kids as opposed to break dancing.

The Road to Destruction and the Effects on the Young Generation

The evolution of this type of music have gone long and far. The generation that is listening to it today is not limited to the ghetto any longer. Its culture and contents have reached across international borders and has affected many. Many of which do not have a clue as to where or how it came about. They are from all races, backgrounds and nationalities. Many of them may still be too young to see or understand that it is only entertainment or why it is tainted with violence. They only hear, see it and like the music. It is these young and impressionable minds that I am concerned about.

They will see and hear some of their favorite entertainers become successful by advocating sex, violence and degrading their women. They will see them with all the nice cars the pretty girls and the money and will try to emulate them.

I must point out that not all rap music and videos are bad. There are a lot of Christian and other decent recordings out there. It is the bad ones that I am concerned about.

Video Game Similarities

Nearly every kid today is rap conscious. Parents I am sure can vouch for that, even though many of them would like not to. My concern is that the kind of rap music and videos that are selling the most today are the ones that have the most violence and sexual overtones in its videos and its lyrics. It appears that sex and violence is the only two things that will sell records today in this upcoming generation. Both can and do sell individually, but when there is a combination of the sorts, it becomes more appealing.

These recordings are played over and over again. We are no longer limited to just our auditory senses when we take in these lyrics, we are now capable of viewing them in music videos. Many of these lyrics are now played out in scenes on a TV screen that can make it seem even more like reality to many in the audience.

I believe that anything that is verbalized or visualized in a negative way over and over again can and will have an affect on young children or weak minds. This feeling is not just limited to the rap industry; it is with any form of medium. I believe it can, and do have an affect young children, especially those who already have young and troubled minds.

If I may digress for just a moment to prove a similar case and point within the entertainment industry that involved a violent video game. Though this may be a little extreme, the causes and effects in my view are very similar in nature.

This one particular news story has grabbed my attention and it is very hard for me to comprehend why anyone would even think of making a game like this one.

Part of the game involves the player entering a police precinct and killing as many police officers as they could by shooting them in the head. To me, this is no different than advocating killing our soldiers, innocent people, and those who protect us.

This act was played out in real life in Fayette, Alabama according to the attorney Jack Thompson who is currently the attorney for one of the relatives of one of the police officers that were killed.

Mr. Thompson has filed a multi-million dollar lawsuit in Alabama against the makers and marketers of Grand Theft Auto, claiming that months of playing the game led a teenager to go on a rampage and kill three men, two of them police officers.

According to Mr. Thompson "What we're saying is that Devin Moore was, in effect, trained to do what he did. He was given a murder simulator," says Thompson.

"He bought it as a minor. He played it hundreds of hours, which is primarily a cop-killing game. It's our theory, which we think we can prove to a jury in Alabama, that, but for the video-game training, he would not have done what he did."

"The video game industry gave him a cranial menu that popped up in the blink of an eye, in that police station," says Thompson "And that menu offered him the split-second decision to kill the officers, shoot them in the head, flee in a police car, just as the game itself trained them to do."

After his capture, Moore is reported to have told police, "Life is like a video game. Everybody's got to die sometime."

In this same article it was noted that David Walsh, a child psychologist who's co-authored a study connecting violent video games to physical aggression, says the link can be explained in part by pioneering brain research recently done at the National Institutes of Health—which shows that the teenage brain is not fully developed.

Does repeated exposure to violent video games have more of an impact on a teenager than it does on an adult?

"It does. And that's largely because the teenage brain is different from the adult brain. The impulse control center of the brain, the part of the brain that enables us to think ahead, consider consequences, manage urges—that's the part of the brain right behind our forehead called the prefrontal cortex," says Walsh. "That's under construction during the teenage years. In fact, the wiring of that is not completed until the early 20s."

Walsh says this diminished impulse control becomes heightened in a person who has additional risk factors for criminal behavior. Moore had a profoundly troubled upbringing, bouncing back and forth between a broken home and a handful of foster families.

"And so when a young man with a developing brain, already angry, spends hours and hours and hours rehearsing violent acts, and then, and he's put in this situation of emotional stress, there's a likelihood that he will literally go to that familiar pattern that's been wired repeatedly, perhaps thousands and thousands of times," says Walsh.

"There's plenty of blame to go around. The fact is we think Devin Moore is responsible for what he did," says Thompson. "But we think that the adults who created these games and in effect programmed Devin Moore and assisted him to kill are responsible at least civilly.

David Walsh, a child psychologist who's co-authored a study connecting violent video games to physical aggression, says the link can be explained in part by pioneering brain research recently done at the National Institutes of Health—which shows that the teenage brain is not fully developed.

Does repeated exposure to violent video games have more of an impact on a teenager than it does on an adult?

"It does. And that's largely because the teenage brain is different from the adult brain. The impulse control center of the brain, the part of the brain that enables us to think ahead, consider consequences, manage urges—that's the part of the brain right behind our forehead called the prefrontal cortex," says Walsh. "That's under construction during the teenage years. In fact, the wiring of that is not completed until the early 20s."

Walsh says this diminished impulse control becomes heightened in a person who has additional risk factors for criminal behavior. Moore had a profoundly troubled upbringing, bouncing back and forth between a broken home and a handful of foster families.

"And so when a young man with a developing brain, already angry, spends hours and hours and hours rehearsing violent acts, and then, and he's put in this situation of emotional stress, there's a likelihood that he will literally go to that familiar pattern that's been wired repeatedly, perhaps thousands and thousands of times," says Walsh.

The makers and supporters of this game may try to use the same argument as the gun makers do, but in my view this is like comparing apples and oranges.

My main issue and concerned with this whole situation is just why would anyone even want to make a video game like that? Why would they want to portray the killing of innocent people and police officers rewarding, even though it is still just a game?

I'm pretty sure that theses engineers and designers would not approve placing pixels or holograms of their sons, daughters, family members and relative in these video games where killing them would reward the players. Then again, probably they would, if it would bring in revenues. These people, many of them well educated and should know better but are simply motivated by money and greed. As far as I'm concerned these people or video game makers are no better than many of the criminals on the streets and should be held liable and treated as such. I believe if you in, "if know better you should do better".

Another case and point which clearly shows a relation to the topic at hand had to do with an Eminem impersonator who beat a woman to death and stuffed her body in a suitcase—a scene reminiscent of the rapper's "Stan" video

Christopher Duncan, 21, has the same hair color, style and tattoos as the rapper Eminem. This Eminem impersonator pleaded guilty to the murder of law student Jagdip Najran.

The 21-year old met Najran at a karaoke evening where she was drawn to him after a performance and took her back to his flat. There he hit her over the head with an iron baseball bat until she was unconscious and stuffed her into a suitcase. Medical experts testified that she remained alive inside the suitcase for at least an hour after being knocked unconscious.

In the Eminem song *Stan* an overly obsessive fan throws his girlfriend into the trunk of his car before driving it over a bridge.
Duncan reportedly told police that he was high on LSD and Ecstasy at the time.

I would be remiss if I do not mention that there are violent overtones, and other moral and ethical issues in other areas of the entertainment industry that needs to clean up their acts. In comparison though, the negative effect that it has compared to those that we are currently facing in the music industry as it relate to the topics at hand will pail when compared to the negative effect of rap on our culture and society, primarily in the inner cities.

The act of advocating violence and aspiring to be a gangster is usually on top of the music charts, if not on the charts that are publicized, it is on the top of the charts in the communities and in the hands of the troubled people.

We went from the some of the more decent pioneers in rap music with groups like the Sugarhill Gang and their number one single Rappers Delight, with innocent lyrics that talks about soggy macaroni, and chicken tasting like wood to Young Geezy's chart topping single Soul Survivor where he talks about selling drugs and disobeying the law.

Young Geezy's chart topping single has lyrics, which goes something like this: "If your looking for me I'll be on the block with my thing (gun) cocked possibly siting on the drop". "If you're looking for me you can find me on the block disobeying law". "Real G bred from the street, pants sagging with my gun in my draws"

Even our record labels, song titles, and group, to include some the self owned production companies must have violent overtones. Titles like Get Rich or Die Trying, group names like Murder Inc. and Ghost Face Killah, and even Def Jam etc.,. These names and connotation does nothing but feed into the negative stereotypes that everyone thinks about this culture.

I would compare some of these rap records, record producers, record companies, and its executives to those of the cigarettes and the big tobacco companies back in the early seventies and eighties. They knew how to target a particular audience and pull them in and get them hooked in order to make millions of dollars.

In this case the cigarettes causes cancer within the body, Gangster rap causes cancer within the communities. At least I can now credit the big tobacco companies because they were smart enough to acknowledge the damages that they were causing and have taken steps to correct the problems and compensate those that were affected. Hopefully one day we will wake up and do the same.

On a brighter note though, as I have mentioned earlier, not all rap is bad, there are a lot of intelligent rappers out there that have great talents and great potentials. The talents and potential of many of these kids wanting to become a famous rapper are enormous.

If they would only focus that love and attention that they have for the music and lifestyle into something less entertaining and more productive. Something like becoming a doctor or a lawyer, which could possibly be even less of a challenge for many of them given the natural talents that some of them are born with and just don't know it.

I have no doubts in my mind that many of them could and would pass any test to be a doctor, lawyer or be someone or do something greater in life if they only had the proper guidance, tools, at their disposal to meet these challenges early on in life.

Many of us from the older generation know that most of it is simply for entertainment purposes only, and will take it as such, however there are still too many more young and even old impressionable minds out there that will view things differently that has, and will become societies problems and continue to pay the price.

I believe that Gangster Rappers TU-PAC and Biggie Smalls were both intelligent entertainers. They were not young, and both of them I believe knew better. Both of them were gunned downed because of their affiliation with the rap industry and its lifestyles.

Was this their own doings, or was it someone else's and why? If we can honestly answer all of these questions, then we should see some of the problems that I'm simply trying to point out. As an African American, I can honestly say that this music culture was one of the last things that we needed right now, especially for those that are living in the inner cities.

This rap trends, lifestyle, or culture; whatever you may want to call it will continue to hurt this sector of people. How long must we continue to make the same mistakes?

It is now hard for me to say that they have never had a chance to pull themselves up and out of trouble and despair, it is much easier now to say that we have never learned quite how to do so.

Comments Made by Bill Cosby

A lot of people had issues with comedian Bill Cosby and what he had to say about our people, which I will commend him for. Bill Cosby's sociopolitical views, especially about the African-American community, are quite complex and have often been reduced to a simplistic representation. Bill Cosby has been critical of Black communities regarding those who hold low standards and allowing fatherless single parent households, high crime rates, and high illiteracy rates. He encouraged ownership of those problems and a more proactive effort from within Black community to fix those problems.

I agree with many of his views and his remarks regarding the decline of the Black American family. It is not that he does not feel the pain. He has been there and done that and has had the courage to stand up and bring attention to real problems that we face.

As an Afro-American male, we have come to a point in time where we are now scared of our own kind than we are of anything else. Many of us do not want to place our kids in schools or live in neighborhoods that are predominantly black. We will sometime go out of our way to avoid our own people, but why? Why are we killing each other abroad and in foreign countries like Africa, parts of the Caribbean and other countries and cities that are solely run by Blacks? Why are so many of us dying of aids? Who can we point the finger at this time? It all boils down to one thing, and the bottom line is that, we have no one to blame for this but ourselves, and until we realize this and take responsibility for our actions nothing will change. It will only get worse.

I remember watching 60 Minutes and saw Ed Bradley do a piece on Howard Stern. They went back to Howard Stern's old neighborhood to see how and where he grew up and how it may have affected him to have made him the person that he is today. It saddened me to hear and see of how he spoke about his mother and his old neighborhood of how it has changed over the years. He spoke about the times when everyone started moving out of his neighborhood because the neighborhood was becoming integrated. His mother thought that it would be a good idea to stay because she believed in integration and thought that everybody was good people and deserved a chance. Then to hear him talk about what he had gone through, as a kid in school was very disappointing to say the least. He talked about the time where he would just be sitting in his classroom, and someone would turn around and punch him in his face for no reason other than the fact that he was white, really sickens me. Unfortunately these kinds of things still go on in many of the schools all over the county.

I remember sitting in class one day when someone in my class fired a paper clip and struck another student in the eye for no apparent reason. That student is now blind in one eye. I did not follow this case to the end but I could probably guess what occurred down the road. Most likely the school has gotten sued and lost its case, the student who shot his classmate in the eye is either dead or in jail, and the female who was shot in the eye is still blind. Sadly there are many more of these cases and other problems within the public school system that needs some drastic changes. There are still a lot of politicians and advocates of these public institutions, however I would bet that many of them would not put their kids in these institutions. I don't blame them though, because I knew that if I had the money I wouldn't either. On a more serious note, there is still plenty of work to be done in these public institutions, which should start with the students in attendance.

Slavery

Slavery is long gone, and over 400 years of slavery is no excuse for us to be killing others or ourselves. Martin Luther king and many other good people have fought and died for justice and many of the things that we now take for granted. They did not nor should not have died in vain. It is beginning to appear that some of the very same people that they gave their lives for in order for them to be able to do the things that they can now do were not worth the sacrifice.

If anything, the fact of just knowing that slavery did exists, and all the pain and losses that we have already gone through and endured, should have been enough to have kept us on the straight and narrow and not resort to what I would call this "madness", that I am seeing today.

Instead of continuing Martin Luther King's dream, we have taken it and turned it into a nightmare, where we have now become our worst enemy.

Though these words are very harsh and cruel, I believe it is necessary in order to grab the attention that we need in order to get us moving again in the right direction. If by chance we all don't get it, or make a move in the right direction after knowing how many of us feel, then those of us who have been identified or called out here should know why. Of course this does not apply to everyone, and only a fool would think so. We know who we are and I believe the American people know who we are.

Millions of our people are still dying all over the world. Whether it because of an illness or by the hands of one of our own, or even someone else's, it is still too many. Thousands, are still being robbed, raped, beaten, murdered and killed in their communities, in their homes, by our own race, and in some cases even their own relative, which makes no sense at all. This just makes you wonder, is it really Nurture or Nature?

Granted these crimes and incidents can and do occur in all races, but no where is it more prevalent than in the black communities. This is by no means limited to the U.S., I cant even begin to talk about the atrocities that are going on in other places like the continent of Africa and other foreign countries that are predominantly run by my people.

If this is not bad enough, we now also have the AIDS epidemic to contend with. We have surpassed every other ethnic group in contracting and succumbing to this virus. Is it that we are just not aware of the dangers of aids, and the other issues, or is it that we just cannot control our desires and ourselves? Are we not able to take the time and effort to try and protect ourselves, our families and or children, or is it that we just don't care?

There may be a combination of factors, but whatever the real reason for these epidemics or series of unfortunate events, if we do not care enough about ourselves, then why should others?

As a good church going person as most us are, we should realize by now that God helps those who help themselves.

Understandingly many of our ancestors were slaves. They could not read nor write and were very poor. They did not have many of the benefits that we now have today. Just under those circumstance we should evaluate ourselves by asking ourselves why? Even though they were dirt poor, and had little or no education, no one was afraid of their own kind as we are today. We were not dying as much or as fast as we are today, despite the injustices of the past. Being poor does not and should not make someone a criminal. It is the freedom to choose that does.

On a brighter note, as I will say from time to time, everyone is an individual and should be judged and treated as such. There are many people of color that are now successful, have done great things, and are continuing to do great things. Many have gone out of their way to help and give back to society and their communities in a positive way.

My only concern is that I'm afraid that many of the efforts that they are putting forth are not as important in the eyes of the beneficiary as it is to those that are concerned.

For someone to have taken their hard earned time and money and give to someone who does not really appreciated it is not the most effective thing to do, simply because the ones who are giving in most cases, were not given or handed anything on a silver platter. These are usually the ones that had to go out and struggle for theirs on their own and there are just too many people in this world that would do better and be more appreciative with just having a chance to wake up in this country. Not to mention many of the immigrants that have migrated to this country like the Koreans, Chinese, and ironically the Nigerians and others who came here with noting and have done well for themselves and continue to make positive contributions to this country.

<u>*My Heroes*</u>

Great people like Bill Cosby, Opra Winfrey, Barak Obama, Dr. Condoleezza Rice, Colonel Powell, Charles Rangel, famous entertainers, even athletes and many others successful people did not get where they are without a lot of hard work, sacrifice and discipline.

The one person that I truly admire within this group is Opra Winfrey. The reason I truly admire her is because she is a great example of someone who has overcome all odds. Going from being a single black female from the south and at one point weighing around 300 lbs., and did not the greatest childhood experiences. She appeared to have had all cards stacked against her. Simply just the ability to have shed all that weight and have kept it off for so long without any type of surgery simply amazes me. She wears her feelings and emotions on her sleeves and is genuine in everything she does. She has done so much and has gone so far despite the many natural and manmade obstacles that were in her path. She has reached out, and in many cases single handedly to help to fix our country's woes. She is the epitome of what a truly successful person consists of or should be, even without the material or financial status. She has truly brought meaning to what it means to succeed despite all odds, and is a true testament to what it is like to be a true American and to live the American dream. If there is a place in the after life where good people go she has definitely earned her place there, and even if there isn't such a place, her legacy will live on in the lives of those that she has touched and many others forever.

No one gets anywhere without hard work, discipline and sacrifice, and if by chance they get there without them, it may be just a matter of time before they lose it all. They may never know what it really took to get there, or how to maintain what they have when they do get there. I believe that part of being satisfied in life is being able to look back at your accomplishments and achievements and see what it took and what was accomplished to get there so we can proudly and honestly say that, "we have been there and have done that".

We cannot all be entertainers and athletes nor should we all aspire to be one. Let us not limit ourselves. There are a countless number of other things that we can do and be in this world during our lifetime to help our country, communities, our fellow man, and ourselves. If by chance we can't find that something, we must find ourselves. If we cannot find either of the two then we must find the lord. If not, he will usually find us a little bit earlier than we have expected.

Time for Change

I would estimate that a good 30 years and trillions of dollars of government assistance have been thrown in many of the problem communities, mainly for education and the bare necessities. We have failed to capitalize on many of these benefits. These benefits were not intended to sustain a comfortable living or lifestyle nor should it have been intended to. The government can only do so much. We are only as good as we want to be, we should all aspire to be something great in life and do something good for our country and each other. We cannot force someone to be all that they can be if he or she does not want to. We can only provide them the tools and, if the tools are not utilized effectively and efficiently, it is still a loss cause. No amount of money can fix someone who does not want to be fixed.

It is now time, and has been for quite some time now for the communities to try and give back by helping to pick themselves, their brothers and sisters, and their communities up and move forward. We must stop this dependency, and stop feeding off each other in a negative way in our communities and aspire to be something great in life. Success depends very little on being given what you want, and much more on becoming the best you can be.

It is not an issue of black on white anymore; it is an issue of black on black. All of us who are African American and living in an urban environment must now live and praise god if our sons, daughters, grand children, and even ourselves will actually make it through the day or get to live to a ripe old age without our lives being scarred, interrupted or ended by one of our own. This is the real issue. We don't need money or the material things to have life; it is life that we need in order to have anything.

I would bet that if anyone were to ask almost any kid from the inner cities who is one of their favorite leaders or role models, the first person that would come to mind would be someone like the rapper Snoop Dog, or the basketball player Michael Jordan, over someone who could make a real difference in their lives.

Where are our all our black leaders now? Are the churches and their pastors trying to help? I'm sure they are, but why must the pastors with the largest congregation live in million dollar mansions and have private jets and preach prosperity on Sundays while the rest of their congregation pay tides and go home happy and their situation is not getting any better. "Your day will come they say", "just be patient", while they live out their lavish lifestyles.

I soon await the days when a cover charge is required to attend services, and Automated Teller Machines (ATMs) are at the front doors to assist in helping us show our patronage to the lord.

We must take a hard look at what is going on. We need not preach prosperity everyday. What we need to be preaching is more about self-reliance, self-discipline and independence, and taking back control of our kids, our families, and our communities and the importance of school and a good education. If we can get this accomplished, then and only then can we have a better chance of prosperity. In my eyes, prosperity should not be measured in terms of monetary values alone as many of us are now doing.

A Typical Day in the City as A Youngster Growing Up

I will now take you on a journey to give you a feel of what is was like on a typical day in the inner cities for me as a youth growing up. Though I was maybe just a little different than most, I have had the same, or possibly even some of the worst experiences compared to my peers as I was growing up. I simply had to make my own choices and decisions on what kind of lifestyle I preferred to live.

Despite what I may say or write about, there are still a lot of good people who are living the projects, the ghettos and the inner cities. It is the overwhelming concentration of some of which I will label from this point on as being, "undesirables" that I have a problem with. We have all at one point our another in life have had an encounter with one of them or may someone who has.

Growing up in the big city was a haven for these undesirables. These people would usually harass, attack, and make people lives miserable for no worthwhile reason at all. They normally like to pick on the weak and defenseless.

As a child growing up I had no tolerance for this type of behavior, and today I'm still not sure why I was that way. I sometimes wonder, could it be that I was born that way? Or could it be of the environment that I was in? Most experts would say it is a combination of environment and my upbringing, but I would lean more towards genetics, as I will make reference to over and over throughout this book. One thing for sure in my case is that it had very little to do with environment.

If I was around and saw a fight I would always be the one to jump in a try to break it up regardless of who was fighting; especially one that involved a bully. If there were a bully on my block, or one that I that I knew somewhere else, I would go out of my way to confront him or her to try to change their ways. At a mere 5'5" I was very small and skinny in stature, I was very physically strong, and fearless. Most kids growing up in the projects at some point becomes fearless. I believe this is why most doing not live past twenty-one years old where I was grew up.

I remember going to what was supposed to be a free party at the community center in my neighborhood. There was a bully at the door that went by the name of Peter Judge. He had his hat in his hand and extended out at the door. He was charging people a dollar to get into the party. In order to get into the party you must place a dollar in his hat as cover charge. The only problem with that is that the function was supposed to be free to all in the community, and no one should have been at the door charging and forcing people to put a dollar in his hat in order to get in.

As he was busy collecting a dollar at the door from everyone who wanted to get in, it was my turn and I walked up to the door. He told me I had to pay him a dollar before I could get in. I told him this was a free function and I was not going pay him a dollar to get in.

The line began to grow as he and I was at a standoff as continued to block me from entering through the door without putting a dollar in his hat. I refused to pay and the line got longer and longer. Onlookers from inside and outside of the center began to gather around. They all looked on as I refused to pay, curious to see what he or I was going to do to settle the dilemma.

I told him to move out of my way a second and then a third time. I braced myself for a physical confrontation as I was waiting to see what his response was going to be. To my surprise he simply moved out of my way and said, "just wait, once I finish here I am going to break your face".

I did not reply back to his comment of breaking my face, I just simply went by and walked back to the dance floor as if it did not matter. It appeared that he was too busy collecting money at the time and it would be a while before he got through collecting money from those still waiting in line before he would get a chance to come to the back of dance floor to break my face.

While at the party his comment of breaking my face never left my mind. I knew that he would eventually confront me and I will have to fight him. As confident as I was back then, I really wanted to fight him, but I would have to wait on him to initiate it like he said he would. My mother use to tell me that you should never hit any one first and that have always stuck with me. My belief was that if your in the right, you cant lose and since I have never lost a fight or gotten beaten up, I was ready to break his face instead.

I stayed until the party was over but to my surprise I did not hear from him or see him again that night. As I left the community center and was walking home that night, I could not help but keep thinking about it. I began to laugh to myself because to me it just seemed so ridiculous. I could not believe that all those people were actually giving him money to enter the free facility simply because they were too scared of what he may have done if they didn't.

It has been over 25 years and I still remember his name and his reputation very well. His reputation was one to be afraid of. He stood about six feet tall and weighed approximately 250lbs. His job or occupation literally was to rob, fight, and beat people up on a daily basis. Rumors were that he might have even shot and killed a couple people, to include a homeless person that was just lying around near a trash dumpsters minding his own business.

These rumors back then were usually more true than false, and even without them this would usually be his method of operation. I was not around to actually be a witness to any of the rumors, however I was there on occasions to witness him in his act of preying on innocent victims that simply wanted to do nothing but go about their business.

In the big city no matter how tough you are there is usually someone tougher than you are. Generally speaking, the crowd that you hang out with is similar in nature and will usually take care of its own within the group for the benefit of society. I will attempt to clarify this statement by saying what I mean is that; if you hang out with a group that commit crimes, it is usually just a matter of time before you will become a crime victim yourself, and the perpetrator is usually someone within the group.

Though he too is classified as one of these undesirables, justice within the group will have been served. In many of the cases they will end up paying the ultimate price with their lives.

Jails for most of them within these types of groups are the easy way out if in there for life. When released they are usually the same repeat offenders, who continue to take their toll on society and destroys and makes others life miserable.

Needles to say that same night Peter Judge was shot several times by one of his buddies they called Little Joe. The word that was out the next day was that he and Little Joe was in some type of dispute in front of the pizza parlor in the neighborhood. Little Joe pulled out a gun and began shooting him and he began to run. He ran into the pizza parlor that was on the corner begging for mercy from the storeowner as Little Joe continued to pump bullets into his body according to eyewitnesses.

The funny thing about it is that I saw little Joe the next day and spoke with him for a minute as he went about his business as if nothing had happened, unaware that he had killed Peter Judge the same night that he said he was going to break my face.

Little Joe was picked up later that day by the police and was charged, convicted and sent to prison for several years.

Now that I think about it 25 Years later as I am writing this book, it simply amazes me to think of how normal it seemed to be living in such a violent environment.

If I was not there to hear and see it in person, it would just be another day in the neighborhood, then again, it was in fact just another day in the neighborhood. This is just one of the many true stories of a typical day in the ghetto. No media coverage or reporters needed here.

My Thoughts on Human Nature and Its Relation to Crime & Ideas on Dealing With It

I was accustomed to seeing fights and crimes almost on a daily basis. I had always been the one who did not like to see people get hurt, and once again, I'm still not sure exactly why this was, given all of the situation and circumstances that I was faced with daily while growing up.

As I did then, and as I do now, I will continue to believe that there should be no room or tolerance for unnecessary violence in this world. I continue to wonder was it due to parental or environmental pressures that have made me more sensitive to violence? Or could it be that the liking of violence is just not in the blood and that I was born with a conscience that is over protective? Or was it because I was an individual that was capable of making my own decisions despite the peer pressures and other outside influences?

Again, I would give more credence to the latter two, due to the fact that neither one of my parent were able to take control of my life as I was growing up. I was fearless at every angle. I could have gone either way, but have always chosen to do right simply because it is the right thing to do and knew that my parents would have wanted me to.

The love and respect that I have for my parents despite any deficiencies that they may or may not have had will always be there. I know that they have done the best that they could, given the situation and circumstances that they had to deal with. In addition, the fact that they were also raising seven kids, six of who were boys, was not an easy task.

Similar to some animals, I believe that we are born with some biological factors, which makes some of us more aggressive than others. The ones that are more aggressive will usually have a tendency to be more violent and disruptive in a civilized society regardless of how much structure was put in place to deter the behavior. When placed in an environment that is less structured our natural animal like instinct to become violent will come to bear.

Without any perceived immediate or long-term negative consequences to our actions, we will attempt to fulfill our desires without remorse. The ability to have a conscience or lack there of, may consist of how much or little of these chemicals, genes, or hormones we may have in our bodies and how they react with our brain.

These biological factors are primarily what make us who and what we are, and capable of becoming civilized human beings. It is what makes us great men and women.

How we use it is affected by internal and external factors. Even though both are important, I tend to lean more towards the internal ones, which is the basis for many of my arguments as you will continue to witness in my writings.

I believe that by raising many of the issues that I talk about in my book, regardless of how true or untrue they may be, can help us to become more efficient and effective at what we do and how we do them.

It is these great men and women of the world with the right biological ingredients, factors, or makeup, as I use interchangeably, and are conscious of these facts is what keeps our world moving in a positive direction.

There are many different readings and studies as it pertains to social science, human behavior, and biology. I do not feel a need to cite any of these readings because many of them are simply only theories as it relates to the issues at hand. The things that I talk about are simply from past learnings, personal observations and past experiences. What we do and why we do them should be simply left to the experts and my readers to prove or disprove. I am no expert. I am only writing about what I think as it relates to why we are what we are, and why we do what we do, which may be totally wrong.

The Good and The Bad

Since the beginning of time there has been a constant battle between good and evil. Great men and women have risen to the occasion and have brought us this far. There is still a majority out there that could care less as to where this world is going or who lives or dies as long as they get what they want. These people are what I would classify as being the forces of evil, or undesirables that we must, and will have to contend with in order to keep this world moving in a positive direction.

These people require special attention. Once identified, they should be separated and afforded the opportunity to be placed within their own little community to live their lives as they please. They should be placed and kept in an environment where they are more suitable among their peers. They should not be placed in an environment where they cannot hurt or affect other people that do not believe in their lifestyle, so that if and when they do choose to hurt someone, it will be those that are more accepting of that kind of lifestyle.

Unfortunately this ideal place may sound similar to our current penal system where many of them eventually will wind up, and will use it only as a revolving door. In order to protect them from themselves, and protect society, we should take a closer into replacing these revolving doors with ones that are more conventional. These individuals can and will only live in a structured environment, where constant monitoring and discipline can be done more efficiently and effectively, which is done best in a controlled and confined environment.

Since replacing the revolving doors are not doable at point in time, in an effort to continue to safeguard society once we do let them out, we must continue to monitor them and treat all these violent and repeat offenders as we now treat child molesters

We have all seen or heard of a crime that may have been prevented by one of these undesirables if only they were still confined.

We are not there yet but we are getting better at working together for change. We must continue to work together to change the laws in order to help remedy the situation, and stop placing our kids, and innocent law-abiding citizens and our families in harms way from these undesirables.

Currently the statistic shows that violent crimes are on the decline which is good, but how many of us actually believes this is true or feels safer today than we were ten, twenty, or thirty years ago. Let's get real people, a lot more has to be done.

As these predators continue take their toll on society today and in the years to come, If we don't do something now, we will be forced to at some point in the future when the damage had already been done. How many more rapes, murders, child abduction and molestation, and other violent crimes must we have by these criminals and repeat offenders before we actually wake up and smell the coffee.

Should we wait until it hits home? Most of us will not get involved until it hits close to home, with a family member, a close friend, a relative, our even ourselves, if we are lucky enough to survive our encounter. Not surprisingly, many of us will wait for it to happen to us first, which is very unfortunate, but as they say; experience can be our best teacher.

Under our current system there is very little we can do to shield ourselves from these predators. Some may think that being wealthy and having plenty of money will save them. It will not; it only shields us to an extent. Not having the freedom or ability to move and go where and when we want and do what we want safely without the perceived burdens of potentially becoming a victim of one of these undesirables' takes away our individual freedoms. This is one of the fundamental building blocks that have made this country great.

We cannot continue to run away from it. It will continue to break down the fabrics of our society. It will find us in some way, form, or fashion no matter where we run. We can run but can't hide. We may not be able to stop it completely at this point and time but we can definitely do some things to slow it down. Crime is like cancer. Like cancer crimes spreads into our communities and surrounding area. It can attack us in places that we never thought possible. We may not yet have the cure for cancer but we can identify it, cut it out or slow it down, and this procedure works best when it is caught early. We can do the same for crime.

Crime and criminals can be found almost everywhere. They come in all shapes, sizes, and can be found at all ages and stages in life. They are from every race, group, and even religion. In other words these undesirables are simply part of the human race and these people will flourish wherever and whenever Big Brother is not there to keep them in check.

Though their crimes may be different in nature the outcome is usually the same, someone has been victimized and punishment should be dealt accordingly regardless of gender or backgrounds. Not to mention domestic violence, which is in itself a whole other book. This type of violence is statistically consistent across racial and ethnic boundaries. However all I will say in reference to this kind of crime is that if we know of anyone who may be in one of these types relationships, lets see if we can help them to get out of it, especially if there are kids involved. There are times we may want to ask ourselves did he or she deserve getting beaten or killed after every effort to advise them or remove them from the abusive situation has failed. Absolutely not, no one deserves it. It is the abusers that we must focus our attention on, and see what we can do to remove him or her from the situation and placed in controlled environment.

Early Signs

The signs are usually there long before many of them are unleashed onto society. We all must go through school whether it is private public. It is there that we get to see the early and obvious signs. Many will be forced into high schools without basic skills that are required simply because it is too early to throw in the towel on them. The professors can only try to curb and do their best to handle and maintain these potential undesirables until they graduate, dropped out of school, or have reached the age where that they may no longer remain in high school.

Once those that are lucky enough to graduate, they either enroll in college or are free and unleashed on society to become, or not become a productive citizen in society. Some will make and attempts to go to college and will soon find out that there is no one there to hold their hands and force them to go to class, then reality finally begins to sinks in. The ill preparation and the wasted years in middle and high school was too much. There is no way they can now hang in there for four years unless they go back to basics, he or she is really physically talented or have a unique skill that is in demand. Then and only then they may have a chance to really learn or bargain their way through four years of college.

As we work to try and fix the problems that we have with crime and many of these undesirables, we must continue to look for viable solutions to head off the derailment of our young ones, even if it may mean removing them from unfit parents. First we must acknowledge and identify that there is a problem. Once identified we must work to first treat the problem, and if we cannot treat it, as in most cases, we must isolate it so that it does not affect anyone else.

Over the years we have expanded and expended an enormous amount of resources in trying to fix many of theses problem without any avail. I think it is now time to isolate the problem.

After these people have reached a certain age and we have exhausted our efforts to try to steer and keep them on the right path and they still choose to do otherwise, we should not be afraid to curb their behavior. If this means locking them up and throwing away the key until they can prove otherwise, it is what we must do. Though this may seem to be a little extreme it is not. It is not that they have not had a chance or an opportunity to do what's right. In most cases they have had far too many chances. By giving them this much freedom, we are taking away our freedoms, which is an injustice for all of us. Let's give someone else a chance that have never had one. The only problem with that is that, in order to find someone who had never had a chance we would have to go outside of our country and bring them here.

More Jails

Until we can break this cycle of perpetual violence we should continue build more jails to put and keep these people. Nearly all of them have been through the penal system several times. Many of them have participated in work release programs and different kinds of rehabilitation and most will have failed to stay out of trouble. We know that it is not possible to keep these people in jail forever at this point and time, but I do know that it is possible that we can keep them in jail for a very long time. We must simply keep them under lock and key until they are no longer capable of inflicting damage on individuals and society.

We continue to release these offenders in hopes that he or she will not offend again. Many of them will go through some sort of work or rehabilitation program prior to being released but we must stop kidding ourselves, most of us know that rehabilitation programs do not work.

It is true that every once in a while we may find someone that is truly rehabilitated but for the most part it does not work. If we ever come across an ex-offender that is truly rehabilitated, I would bet that it would not have been due to attending or enrolling in the standard rehabilitation program.

The truly rehabilitated will find it in themselves within their hearts and soul to do it on their own without the need for a program. In most cases they will have to have had a life or death encounter, truly hit rock bottom, or truly find the lord, and very few ever make this cut. Even if they do, it is not significant enough to continue to expend our manpower and resources.

If they truly want out they will find it within themselves on their own which is always the best way because help cannot be there when their all alone an have to make a decision.

Most will return to the streets and to commit more crime and revert back to their old ways. I believe the risks are still too great because there are far too many more innocent people out there that are more willing and important to worry about that would love to have a chance to do the right thing and become a productive citizen.

It is time for us to take a bold stand and draw the line. It is time to stop wasting our tax dollars and stop putting innocent lives at risk. Continuing to release these repeat offenders to affect society over and over again makes absolutely no sense. Keeping these offenders behind bars will benefit everyone in the long run, to include the offenders themselves.

If we feel guilty about this idea, then perhaps an alternative measure could be to build a bigger and better society for them behind bars where they can live out their sentences among their peers in a controlled environment, as I have stated earlier. By creating an environment were they are more comfortable and suitable among their peers can relieve them of the responsibility and the pressures of having to conform as required in a free and civilized society.

Another option for those who think this form of containment may be too harsh or inhumane may be to establish a very large community outside of prison where they can live among themselves when they are released. Some may have already witnessed something to this effect, however in order for something like this to work, and work properly will require further studies and an abundance of resources.

Once or if this is ever established and they decide to leave this community, they should be registered in an offender's registry and wear some type of tracking device prior to leaving that community so that they can be monitored. If possible, preferably some type of implantable non-removable microchip or a similar electronic or traceable device that will follow them to the grave.

If all that I have talked about so far has not yet grab some attention and upset many of my readers, then my job is not done.

Though this may sound far-fetched, it is not. Just imagine if we could track and monitor every criminal as to where they go, or where they have gone, or where they have been. If a crime is committed and we have probable cause to suspect that this individual is or was involved in the crime and has one of these non-removable traceable devices on his or her person, then we could simply rewind the tape, if you will, just to see where and when he or she has been in the area of the crime or crime scene.

I know that we are capable of this technology. It is just a matter of when, how, and if we can do this without violating individual's rights and all the other issues that will normally surface with it. I would be one the first to volunteer if we do adopt such a policy if it is proven safe, and would only be used for its intended purpose, which is to curb crime and find criminals.

Just think if this became a reality, oh what a deterrent this would be for those who commit some of the most serious crimes.

In fact there is already a corporation called Digital Angel with this similar kind of technology that I had in mind. Digital Angel Corporation engages in the development and deployment of sensor and communications technologies that enable the identification, location tracking, and condition monitoring people, animals, and objects. It operates in two segments, Animal Applications and, GPS and Radio Communications. The Animal Applications segment develops, manufactures, and markets a line of electronic and visual identification devices for the companion animal, livestock, laboratory animal, fish, and wildlife markets worldwide. This segment principally employs electronic ear tags and implantable microchips that use radio frequency transmission. The GPS and Radio Communications segment designs, manufactures, and supports global positioning systems enabled equipment for location tracking and message monitoring of vehicles and aircraft in remote locations, as well as for telemetry, mobile data, and radio communications applications.

No doubt this is a very controversial subject, but my take on it is that if we have noting to hide then we should not be too concerned. If we ever get so far as implementing this procedure I would recommend that we first start with murderers, child molesters, and other violent and repeat offenders. These people specifically because they have already abused their rights and I do not believe they should be afforded the same rights as everyone else. They have used and abused whatever privileges they have had in a civilize society. They have had their chances, and instead of using it to their benefits, they have chosen to use it to take away the rights and freedom of others.

It does not and should not mater what race, religion ethnicity etc; we are all part of the human race. Many of these people simply do not have the biological makeup to function in a truly civilized and free society as I have pointed out on several occasions.

Many experts will argue that violence is caused by environmental factors but my life experiences have lead me to believe differently. A more viable and acceptable answer would be that there is a combination of both, however if the environment is not there, we must choose to do what comes naturally and then we must ask ourselves what would we do if no one was watching.

If environmental factors were solely the case then why is it so hard for many of us to be rehabilitated. There were three things that I have mentioned earlier that I think could truly turn someone around. Like I have said earlier, unless there is a chemical or biological change within the body, or something truly spiritual or devastating occurs in their lives, in most cases it is too hard or nothing really changes. (1) As far as changing or biological makeup, we not cannot do. (2) As far as predicting a tragedy or traumatic event, we cannot do. (3) As far as trying to make someone truly find the lord, we cannot do. Only the lord can do either or any of these three things and it may take a combination of the fist two in order to get to the third. The best that we can do for them and ourselves is to place them in a controlled environment or simply just hope for the best.

I know this may sound cruel, insensitive, and is a very hard fact to swallow. However we must all come to realize that these people are out there. Simply turning our heads and ignoring that a problem do exist will cause many more good people to want to throw in the towel like so many of us have already done.

Going to the Root of the Problem

Many of these undesirable are usually well past the stage for rehabilitation because learning the difference between right and wrong and good and bad usually begins in the home with the parents. However it is ultimately the individual that will make the final call on what he or she will or will not do.

Parents have and will always be our primary teachers and our first line of defense. If that link is weak or broken or was not there, unless we are truly born leaders, we will have a hard time fending for ourselves unless someone steps in and assume that weak or broken link early on in life.

If there is a problem with the parent or guardian then most likely there will be a problem with the child. The child will in turn pass those good or bad habits, traits, or links on to his or her offspring and so forth and so on.

This pattern continues to recycle itself until some type of positive intervention occurs or that link disappears. However no matter how broken the link may be, when it applies to serious deviant behaviors as it relates committing serious crimes, simply does not and should not hold water.

With the potential for genetic engineering being considered, there are plenty of discussions of how much of the way children turn out is contributed to their genes, and how much comes from the way they are brought up. There are strong arguments on both sides and it is most likely that the final result will be a combination of the two as I have already stated several times.

Many of us have worked with kids, especially those who work with them in the earlier stages in life, such as the preschools and nurseries. It is impossible to ignore the fact that the sensible, polite, caring children do generally seem to have sensible, polite, caring parents, and the more disturbed the home life, the more we see emotional and behavioral problems in those children.

Regardless of this fact, each one of these kids throughout their long journey into adulthood is taught the difference between what is right and what is wrong. If it was not taught by the parents, then simply by their interaction with other children or society itself, possibly by trial and error, or just simple observation. If it was not learned throughout that long journey to adulthood then maybe he or she is truly exceptional and may truly need that special attention. If so there are plenty of facilities that are better suited for this type of individual.

Unless we are mentally handicapped or incapacitated, regardless of what type of parent or guardian he or she have had while growing up, by the time a child reaches his early or late teens, and is old enough to go to college, he or she have had more than enough life experiences to know right from wrong.

There is simply no excuse. I was able to see it in my pre teen years without any supervision, and under some of the worst conditions. It is, and will continue to be very difficult for me to see and understand why it is so hard for others with the exception of the mentally handicapped to grasp this concept. The only logical explanation for all the wrong doers in this world is that in actuality, they will know in their hearts and minds what is right and wrong, but only chooses to do what is in their best interest at the moment.

The ability to reason and control ones mind and body in order to suppress many of our instincts is what makes us human beings that are capable of living in a civilized society. If the mind is not strong enough to suppress these instincts, then we must make it to where the desired benefits and the effects of achieving those benefits are weighed heavily.

The perceived benefits vs. the repercussion of the act or acts are weighed prior to making our decisions. Simply guaranteeing an unpleasant form of repercussion, or adverse action will usually deter those of us who are not mentally handicapped but insist on doing wrong.

Decisions are made depending on the risk factors, and the tolerance levels associated with the physical and biological makeup of each of us as individuals. They can vary widely and are carefully weighed prior to performing any act. If our penal system were to respond in kind as is relates to the type of violent crimes that each perpetrator has committed on his or her victim, this would significantly reduce violent crimes. Someone who shoots someone in the head and kills them and then burns their bodies would definitely think twice before he or she commits this type of crime if they were a 100% sure if they were caught they would have the same done to them. Though we could compare it to bringing back the guillotine or public hangings, but at this point in time I don't think a lot of people would have a problem with it if it would deter these criminals. We can all agree that these are what we may call forms of cruel and unusual punishment, however I do believe it was effective in preventing crimes during its time. Weighing this against the possibility of getting a lethal injection, going to jail for life and still being able to watch TV, participate in recreational activities, get free medical care, have three meals a day and even go to school if they like. It is almost surprising why many more don't volunteer to go to prison rather than trying to find a job. After all, it would be the same thing that they were doing before they went to jail anyway, with only the exception of not being able to do some of those things with the opposite sex. Going to jail is simply a vacation for most criminals. I have worked there as a correction officer and I know what life is like in there.

The individuals that fall into this category cannot be part of a truly free and civilized society and do not make great leaders. Though they may not be mentally challenged, he or she will most likely have some of the biological makeup that would place him or her in the category that will need some type of supervision at the very least, or restraints at the very extreme.

We know that as infants we are all self-serving individuals and our natural instincts to survive is at the forefront. Naturally some kids are more aggressive than others are and the males are usually more aggressive than the females. We must all go through some kind of socialization process in order to live in society as civilized human beings.

Naturally by placing a woman in charge of our country would strive for a more caring, honest, safer and less violent world simply because of their physical composition. However whether or not she is capable of doing it is strictly due to the resistance and the opposition she would have to contend with from her male counterparts in and outside of our country. In time though I do believe we can have a women president, but not right now. The world is still too much of a dangerous place.

The struggle for life and power and dominance is simply in our nature. It is a constant struggle for survival of the fittest, even though the fittest does not necessarily means the best. Must we subdue or kill our enemy and have the winner takes it all mentality? Could it be that killing is also another way of nature taking care of itself in order to keep the supply and demand and the balance of nature in check?

We can argue on these issues if we like. How true or untrue these explanations may be, it should not stop us from making this world a more fair, equitable and better place to live for generations to come. In fact, due to our abilities to reason and understand some of these facts or fallacies if you wish, can explain some of my cynical and non-cynical views. Our human intelligence far surpasses what we once thought were impossible and our abilities to defy nature is what makes us humans that are capable of living in a civilized society.

We can now make what we use to call the impossible happen, even if that means disrupting nature. Our ability to intervene, counteract and combat some of the natural occurrences of nature as it relates to many of the illnesses, diseases, and natural disasters that are thrown at us is simply amazing. Many of us would have followed in the path of the dinosaurs and succumb to the many forces of nature if it were not for our intelligence. Our bout with nature will not be the first nor will it the last time. The best that we can do with the limited time that we have on earth is try and make it a better place to live.

Our days are limited here and we are simply just like specs of sand in time and space, compared to that of Mother Nature and its forces. During our time here, it is very important that we do the best that we can by protecting our ecosystem and ourselves for future generations to come. At the blink of an eye we know what Mother Nature can do, as witnessed by the tsunami and all the other natural disasters and incidents that have occurred just in the last decade.

The laws of nature do not discriminate nor should we. It is the great leaders who have recognized and are aware of these facts that have carried us thus far. It is very easy to destroy mankind in this world but not so for destroying the world. The earth and our solar system will eventually cleanse itself of whatever havoc or toxins we have bestowed upon it and rejuvenate itself even if all life forms are extinct. It may take it a year, a hundred-years or even millions of years. Conversely, we cannot do the same. Comparatively speaking we are just here for a split second in time, so lets make the best of it. Let us allow those who are fortunate enough to be here for that split second in time enjoy their stay here in peace.

Going back to the particular topic as it relates to crime is not a new one new. Our forefathers have laid the groundwork that has been in place for hundreds of years. We have built on it in order make our country a better place live. Some people my still be asking themselves as to who has the authority to decides what is a crime, or who is to say what is right from wrong. Though what is considered a crime can be based on a number of factors, however choosing to do what is right from wrong as it relates to the crimes that I am concerned about is not a difficult task. In the interest of time I will try to keep it simple in defining what I consider a crime; "If a reasonable person can argue whether the act in question is a crime or not, then this is not one of my main concerns".

My Observation as A Correctional Officer

I have had the rear opportunity to work with a mixture of inmates in a maximum-security prison. I was assigned to the Ellis—I unit in the city of Huntsville, Texas which housed some of the most violent criminals to include those that were on death row. Having had the opportunity to work and talk to many of the inmates there, they all had one thing in common. They all claimed to be innocent.

After they have served a majority of their time and are in line to be released, other inmates and correction officers alike would jokingly take bets as to when each of them will return to prison after being released. It was not surprising if we saw the same face return within a couple of weeks or even days after being released. To be honest, trying to predict how long it would be before they would return was truly anyone's guess. However in most cases it was not a matter of if they would return, it was just simply a matter of when.

The recidivism rates of these criminals are very high. Here are just some of the statistics that were taken by the U.S. Department of Justice Bureau of Justice Statistics.

Recidivism of Prisoners Released in 1994

Reports on the rearrest, reconviction, and reincarceration of former inmates who were tracked for 3 years after their release from prisons in 15 States in 1994. The former inmates represent two-thirds of all prisoners released in the United States that year. The report includes prisoner demographic characteristics (gender, race, Hispanic origin, and age), criminal record, types of offenses for which they were imprisoned, the effects of length of stay in prison on likelihood of rearrest, and comparisons with a study of prisoners released in 1983.

Highlights include the following:

- Released prisoners with the highest rearrest rates were robbers (70.2%), burglars (74.0%), larcenists (74.6%), motor vehicle thieves (78.8%), those in prison for possessing or selling stolen property (77.4%), and those in prison for possessing, using, or selling illegal weapons (70.2%).

- Within 3 years, 2.5% of released rapists were arrested for another rape, and 1.2% of those who had served time for homicide were arrested for homicide.

- The 272,111 offenders discharged in 1994 had accumulated 4.1 million arrest charges before their most recent imprisonment and another 744,000 charges within 3 years of release.

By the time most of these convicts get out of jail most would have learned how to become better criminals and be better prepared to avoid getting caught again while serving his or her time in these institutions. When and if they do get caught again and return to prison, in most cases the crime that they have committed will be similar in nature, and more serious than their first time.

If given a choice, my recommendation is to keep these individuals in a controlled environment where they can no longer hurt themselves or those in society. If we feel guilty about it, then there may be other solutions, some of which I have already mentioned on several occasions.

The economist and legal scholar Michael K. Block, who believes that American sentencing policies are still not harsh enough, offers a straightforward explanation for why the United States has lately incarcerated so many people: "There are too many prisoners because there are too many criminals committing too many crimes." Indeed, the nation's prisons now hold about 150,000 armed robbers, 125,000 murderers, and 100,000 sex offenders enough violent criminals to populate a medium sized city such as Cincinnati. Few should dispute the need to remove these people from society.

Since many of us are not willing to remove these people from society forever, if we must let them out, then we must ensure they are registered and monitored forever.

The authorities and the public should be aware of their every move. They should be restricted from living in certain areas and not allowed the freedom to do what ordinary law abiding citizens do, because that they are not.

If I may say again, life is too short and there are too many people in this world that would do anything just to have had the chance and opportunities that these people have had prior to choosing their actions and lifestyle.

My Recommendations on Helping to Reduce Crime

My thoughts and recommendation for starters on how we can assist in reducing crime and cut back on the revolving door syndrome is to issue longer jail sentences and stiffer punishment to criminals. Though all crimes are bad and should not be tolerated, my main focus is on the more serious crimes that involve assaulting or injuring others and those that involve children. These crimes are those that all civilized society should not tolerate under any circumstance.

Sure we are all human and we all make mistakes, and we should learn from them, however some mistakes we cannot afford to make, and for the most part, most first offenders do have an opportunity to redeem themselves under the current penal system.

My recommendations are solely my opinion and if noting else, it is designed to grab some attention.

1. First we should all push for swifter, stiffer and longer jail sentences for anyone who is not a first offender.

2. We must keep the laws very simple so that everyone can understand, including the perpetrators.
   I would keep everything 20/20 clear, concise and easy to understand.

3. There should be a mandatory 20-year jail sentence for someone who as committed a felony for a second time that does not include bodily injury.

4. There should be a mandatory 20+20 more, (40) year jail sentence for someone who has committed a felony for a second time that includes serious bodily injury.

5. There should be a mandatory life or death sentence for someone who has committed or attempted murder other than in self-defense, life for the attempt and death for the act of carrying it out.

Only exception here should be given to juveniles, but if we can prove that they have had the mental capacity to know right from wrong when it comes to taking someone's life and have done so intentionally, they too need to serve life in prison. We must not be afraid to punish these juveniles because after all, it is these same juvenile that grows up to reek havoc on our society. The laws for juvenile as we have it now is entirely too light.

Simply the point that I am trying to make here is that, if I were a criminal, I would not want to be anywhere close to a place that would honestly enforce these laws. Especially with the possibility that there may still be a corrupted official or two that may still be enforcing the law.

Three Strikes and Your Out

The three strikes and your out initiative was a very good idea. However by time the perpetrator finally gets caught the 3rd time and given the sentence that he or she truly deserves, there is no telling how many innocent lives he or she has already affected or destroyed prior to getting arrested for the 3rd time.

This law when applied and used correctly can help to make a difference. The key is to ensure that it is enforced and enforced fairly. We must also ensure that the officials carry out their duties and a responsibility in a professional manner at all times.

There is nothing worse than corrupted official working in a corrupt system. We must ensure those who are prosecuted are prosecuted fairly. Ensure those that are in government and are responsible for enforcing the law do not abuse it. Whenever we suspect or catch one of any of these officials to include police officers and the likes, we must bring it to light and ensure that he or she is prosecuted to the fullest extent of the law, as they are even more deserving of a stiffer punishment for breaching and abusing the public trust than the criminal themselves.

About Crime and My Visions of A Better Tomorrow

Ever wonder what it would be like to live in a crime free city or community. Yes, just imagine a city or community where your kids can go outside and play without having to worry about their safety. In a community where you can go out and leave your house door unlocked or door wide open and not have to worry about an intruder, a burglary or possibly a home invasion. A place where you can drive your vehicle and park it with the keys still in the ignition, leave your wallet or pocketbook on the car seat and not have to worry about returning to your vehicle and seeing broken glass on the ground next to your car windows, someone stealing your car, or your wallet or pocketbook still being there when you return.

Unfortunately it is very hard for some of us to even imagine or think that this is possible. My goal is to get as many people like you to see if we can once again return to a time where we can do these things. If we automatically say or think that we cant, then this further validates a lot of the issues that I talk about in my book.

Crime affects everyone and eventually there will be no place to hide even for the fortunate ones. I am working to come up with an organization called crimefreecity.com. It is an organization that is working to help make our communities safer. Visit us www.crimefreecity.com. Everyone is welcome to contribute by voicing his or her opinions. Together we can help pave the way to creating the first crime free community that we can all live in and be proud of.

Simply just by voicing our opinions on what we think about the current state of affairs as it relates to crime will generally have a tendency generate interest from others that are also concerned. It will create and environment that is unattractive to wrong doers and attract those with similar interest in mind which will help to reduce crime in whichever state or locality or community that adopts it.

We all want to get away from crime and the people who are committing them. We all want real justice and an end to the mockery that is being made of our justice system, as I will explain in this most recent case in Georgia.

A most recent case that has caught my attention in the state of Georgia was for the 27-year-old Jonesboro fast-food worker came on the sixth anniversary of the Nov. 8, 1999, killings. Authorities say Harris abducted 22-year-old Whitney Land and her daughter, Jordan, from Panhandle Park in Clayton County, drove Land's car to Gwinnett County, shot them, put their bodies in the trunk and then burned the vehicle. The 27-year-old Jonesboro fast-food worker was sentenced to life in prison without parole. I think many would agree that crime like this one is so heinous that the only appropriate punishment was death.

The family members for the victims were very upset when the sentence was pronounced and understandably so. The victims are dead and the lives of the family members are destroyed. Mr. Harris get to live approximately 50 more years watching TV, going to school, attending arts and crafts classes, exercising, gets three meals a day everyday, and free medical care. Mr. Harris may be better off now than he was prior to getting sent to prison. At the very least I think the decision to sentence Mr. Harris or any other suspect to life or death once found guilty, the victims relatives and family members, should have a choice in the sentencing phase not only the Jury. In my eyes Mr. Harris and many others like him simply got away with murder, though they may still be spending the rest of their lives in jail.

There are plenty more Mr. Harris's in this world and there are many more Whitney Lands cases. If we want to help and prevent more of them we must all take a stand and try to become active in or government.

Writing letters to our media organizations, local governments, congressman and political party members is a start. How else will they ever know how or what we really feel about anything. If we want change then we should consider letting those who have the power know so that they can try to do something about it.

If the government cannot protect the people then the people should be afforded the opportunity to protect themselves. I commend the state of Florida for their stance on gun laws.

Florida law already lets residents defend themselves against attackers if they can prove they could not have escaped. A new law allows them to use deadly force even if they could have fled and says that prosecutors must automatically presume that the would-be victims feared for their lives if attacked.

We should take this even a step further and extend this law by giving the regular citizens the power to arrest and use deadly force if necessary during the commission of a crime if and when not only their lives are at stake, but during the commission of a crime and when someone else's life is at stake as well.

I favor adopting this policy because we all know that most predators will prefer to victimize the weak and the most vulnerable. These people may choose not to retaliate in kind, or simply just don't have the ability to defend themselves.

By empowering the good citizens of this nation so that they may rise up and combat these undesirables will help make this country and our communities a safer and better place to live. We must not be afraid to stand in unity because in doing so we will help send a clear message to everyone to include those that are coming to this country looking for a better place to live that we operate as one. As we continue to welcome those coming to our country, we must continue to secure and monitor our borders. However we should begin to treat it more seriously to ensure that we only allow those in who are here to make a positive contribution to our country and deport those who are here to do us harm.

The control of criminals is the duty and responsibility of government. The degree or amount of crime in any city or community is a direct reflection on government's ability and willingness to control crime. By the introduction of sound reasonable laws, which can be implemented and enforced, education and the fostering of good social behavior from citizens will follow.

There are three main elements that are used for the control of crime and criminals.

1.   The police: Investigation of crime and capture of criminals

2.   The judicial system: Trial and sentencing of criminals

3.   Correctional services: Punishment of criminals

It is every citizen's constitutional right to be free of crime and live safety. It is the responsibility of government to ensure that this is possible. It is your right to expect that government take notice of the current sad state of affairs and put its house and our house in order.

Criminology is the scientific study of crime. It seeks to find the causes and cures by studying crime and all that influence crime. There often are no simple answers because we come from a diverse range of cultures and beliefs that all to some degree influence crime.

There is always debate on the causes of crime. There are many theories that exist on the influences of reduced or increased crime rate observations. From capture and punishment to the soundness and form of legislation. From the criminal behavior to the motivation of society.

One of the founders of modern criminology, a man with great insight on the control of crime was Cesare Beccaria who had some profound words of wisdom. Some of his theories have been embraced by legislation and many have not.
Much of what Cesare Beccaria wrote in "On Crimes and Punishments" in 1764 still holds true today.
Beccaria's work has become the foundation on which many criminology theories use to build and expand on.

On the prevention of crime; Crimes are more effectively prevented by the certainty than the severity of punishment. The more promptly and the more closely punishment follows upon the commission of a crime, the more just and useful it will be. It is better to prevent crimes than to punish them. This is the fundamental principle of good legislation.

He gave nine principles that need to be in place in order to effectively help in preventing crime. To prevent crime a society must;

1. make sure laws are clear and simple,

2. make sure that the entire nation is united in defense,

3. laws not against classes of men, but of men,

4. men must fear laws and nothing else,

5. certainty of outcome of crime,

6. member of society must have knowledge because enlightenment accompanies liberty,

7. reward virtue,

8. perfect education,

9. direct the interest of the magistracy as a whole to observance rather than corruption of the laws.

If these nine principles were followed there would be less of a need to follow the other principles of trial and punishments.

Feeling safe and secure is one of the most important issues to Americans these days. Feeling safe and secure is one of the most important issues to Americans these days. We not only now have to worry about terrorist, but we also have to worry about it from our own people own in or own neighborhoods as well.

The contents below were provided by Sperling BestPlaces http://www.bestplaces.net, which provides some of America's best and worst cities for crime. It identifies certain cities with an especially high rate of violent crime to include the specific types of crimes. Nassau-Suffolk County NY is among the lowest and has one of the highest paying police departments in the nation. Not to say that there is any correlation with officer's salary and grime rate, but it may need some looking into.

The research team at Sperling's BestPlaces have recently released FBI Uniform Crime Reports to identify those U.S. cities with the highest and lowest rates of crime during 2002. The FBI's Crime Index rate reflects the total number of offenses per 100,000 residents. According to the FBI, the national Crime Index rate for 2002 was 4,118. The Northeast region of the United States had the lowest Crime Index rate of the four regions, with 2,889 offenses per 100,000 residents. The next lowest region was the Midwest, with a rate of 3,883 offenses. The Western region followed with a rate of 4,418 offenses, while the Southern region showed the highest crime rate of 4,722 offenses.

Best Large Cities for Crime (More than 500,000 pop.)

New Jersey boasts three of the nation's safest and most secure cities.
1. Nassau-Suffolk, NY*
Nassau-Suffolk has the second-lowest overall crime rate in the nation, thanks to extremely low violent and property crime rates.
2. Middlesex-Somerset-Hunterdon, NJ
The Middlesex-Somerset-Hunterdon area has one of the lowest murder rates in the nation, in addition to a very low rate of larceny.
3. Ventura, CA
Ventura has a very low property crime rate and one of the lowest larceny rates in the country.
4. Monmouth-Ocean, NJ
Monmouth-Ocean has one of the lowest auto theft rates in the country and an overall low rate of property crime.
5. Bergen-Passaic, NJ

Bergen-Passaic has especially low rates of forcible rape and larceny.

Worst Large Cities for Crime

Although Arizona has two of the most crime-ridden cities in the nation, their violent crime rates are relatively low.
1. Tucson, AZ
Tucson has one of the highest property crime rates in the country, especially larceny. On the bright side, Tucson has a low murder rate.
2. Memphis, TN-AR-MS*
Residents of Memphis contend with the nation's second-highest violent crime rate. In addition, the rate of robbery and burglary are among the nation's highest.
3. Miami, FL
Miami's violent crime rate is the highest in the nation, with especially high incidences of robbery and assault. Thankfully, the murder rate is relatively low.
4. Phoenix-Mesa, AZ
Phoenix-Mesa has one of the highest rates of auto theft in the nation.
5. Little Rock-North Little Rock, AR
The Little Rock area has a high rate of property crime, especially larceny.

Best Medium Cities for Crime (200,000–500,000 pop.)

New England seems to be an especially safe and secure region.
1. Danbury, CT
Danbury has lowest overall crime rate in the nation, as well as the lowest property crime rate.
2. Stamford-Norwalk, CT
Second only to its neighbor Danbury, the Stamford-Norwalk area has one of the lowest property crime rates in the U.S.
3. Johnstown, PA
Johnstown has an especially low rate of property crime. The murder rate is a bit higher than one might expect but is still well below the U.S. average.
4. Dutchess County, NY
Dutchess County has a very low burglary rate, which helps contribute to low overall rate of property crime.
5. Portsmouth-Rochester, NH-ME
The Portsmouth-Rochester area has low rates of property and violent crime, but there is a significant rate of forcible rape.

Worst Medium Cities for Crime

The South seems to be particularly challenged with crime.
1. Myrtle Beach, SC
Myrtle Beach has the highest total rate of crime in the nation, due to a high rate of violent crime and the nation's highest rate of property crime. In particular, the rates of assault, burglary and larceny are particularly high.
2. Montgomery, AL
The murder rate is significantly high in Montgomery, as are the rates of robbery, burglary and larceny.
3. Laredo, TX
While the larceny rate is high in Laredo, residents can take comfort in the relatively low rates of murder and forcible rape.
4. Waco, TX
Like Laredo, violent crime is less of a concern in Waco than property crime. In particular, burglary and larceny are a problem.
5. Wilmington, NC
Wilmington has the second-highest rate of burglary in the country. On the other hand, the rates of forcible rape and assault are low.

Best Small Cities for Crime (Less than 200,000 pop.)

1. State College, PA
State College has low crime rates across the board. In particular, the burglary and auto theft rates are among the nation's lowest.
2. Steubenville-Weirton, OH-WV
Property crime is especially low in the Steubenville-Weirton area, especially the rate of larceny.
3. Wheeling, WV-OH*
While property crime is extremely low in Wheeling, the rates of murder and assault are a bit higher than might be expected.
4. Pittsfield, MA*
Pittsfield has not only one of the lowest murder rates in the nation, but also an exceptionally low rate of larceny. However, the rate of forcible rape is significant.
5. Wausau, WI
Like Pittsfield, Wausau's rates of murder and larceny are among the nation's lowest. The violent crime rates are also low.

Worst Small Cities for Crime

1. Topeka, KS
Topeka has the highest rate of property crime among cities with fewer than 200,000 residents. The rates of larceny and robbery are especially high.
2. Pine Bluff, AR
Pine Bluff has a high rate of murder and the ninth-highest rate of robbery in the nation.
3. Monroe, LA*
Monroe suffers from significant property and violent crime, especially assault and larceny.
4. Alexandria, LA
Alexandria has the fourth-highest violent crime rate in the nation. Murder and assault are a problem, in particular, but the rate of forcible rape is low.
5. Florence, SC
Assault and larceny rates are high in Florence, but the murder rate is low.

Methodology

The FBI's Uniform Crime Reporting Program Crime Index was used for this study. This index consists of the combined rate of murder and nonnegligent manslaughter, forcible rape, robbery, assault, burglary, larceny and auto theft per 100,000 population. This study considered 331 United States Metropolitan Statistical Areas. The data was taken from the FBI's Uniform Crime Reporting Program report for 2002.

*The following cities did not report crime statistics to the FBI in 2002, so 2002 rates were estimated based on previous years' local statistics and current year's city, state and county data: Nassau-Suffolk, NY; Memphis, TN; Monroe, LA; Wheeling, WV-OH; Pittsfield, MA. To view the complete findings and crime rates for all 331 metro areas, visit Sperling's BestPlaces.net website at www. bestplaces.net/2002crime.html.

Leaving the Neighborhood

I will now take you on a journey from the streets to the boardroom to the military. The choices that I have made in order to feel and think the way I do have were fostered throughout my career as a believer in fighting for those who could not fight for themselves.

While trying to better myself and realizing that there was not much for me to do in my community I enrolled in college and attempted to get a degree in business. While in college I landed a job in an advertising agency where I worked in order to take care of some of my bills while going through school. I did not particularly like this field of work. It appeared as though I did not fit in. The environment seemed like it was just too soft and safe, not sure exactly why, but I knew that I had always wanted to become a police officer but I was still too young at the time and this was just not the place. I enrolled in the Army's delayed entry program, which required that I went into the military once I have graduated. I eventually graduated and left home and thought when I returned I would be old enough to take the police exam to become a police officer.

I left home in June of 1984 for the first time. I was away from home for the first time in my life and ended up in an environment that was much different than what I was accustomed to. Prior to leaving New York I was never yelled at or forced to do anything by anyone.

My first stop after leaving New York was Kentucky for basic training where for the first time I saw a lot of white faces. We were picked up by a bus from the airport and taken to the training base at Fort Knox. I stepped off the bus with three large suitcases and a duffel bag. The first thing that the Drill Sergeant said to me as I stepped off the bus with my three bags was "where the hell are you from?" I told him New York Sir, he replied, "New York!" "I am a dam Drill Sargent, Not a Sir!" "Where the hell do you think you are going with all those bags, on a vacation?" Do you think this is a golf resort? I did not reply, all I could do was hold back a smile. He then told everyone to grab his or her bags and run to the in-processing station, which was approximately a quarter mile away. I thought it was all a joke. I never quite knew how to take it because I had never had anyone stand and yell in my face like that.

I saw some of the other recruits laughing and smiling as I was getting yelled at until he turned and gestured as if he was going to jump on one of them for smiling. I grabbed my bags and began running to try to catch up with the crowed that he had already instructed to take off running. The drill sergeant ran and stood behind me to ensure that every time I would stumble or drop one of my bags I would pick it up immediately and continue to run. For the 8 weeks of basic training this one drill sergeant gave me hell the entire time. But now that I look back at it, it was probably the best thing that he could have ever done. However if knew better I would never have told him I was from New York. They do not take too kindly of folks from the big cities for some reason. I now understand why.

After basic training we were placed in a classroom environment to learn and train on the M-1 Abrams Tank. There I had first real interaction with working closely with other people of different races in a classroom environment. There were people of different nationalities and backgrounds than what I were use to. It taught us how to associate and assimilate in a totally different environment. This 16 weeks of training gave us the necessary skills and tools that were required to become responsible individuals. It instilled discipline in us, and made me understand the meaning of values, loyalty, respect, selfless service, honor, integrity and personal courage and all the other good thing that simply makes us good people. Some of which many of us may have had instinctively in varying degrees and brought them to the forefront.

It gave us what I taught at the time was many of the necessary ingredients and attributes of a leader, which begins with some of the basic principles of leadership like first getting to know yourself and then seeking self-improvement. Some people are natural leaders as I have stated on many occasion, however most people must be trained to become leaders. It taught us to adhere to moral principles, to seek and take responsibility for our actions, and many more on the principles of leadership that helps to make us all good leaders and become better people. From that point on I have taken all the information that I have learned built on it and became a true soldier.

My Military Journey and the War in Iraq

Having had the opportunity to serve in the military and work with young soldiers from all backgrounds and walks of life, have proven to me that almost anyone regardless of where they are from can do almost anything if they put their minds into it regardless of what they were exposed to early in life.

Even though those early experiences may or may not give them an advantage, whatever task is at hand, if he or she is given a set of rules or standards to follow and achieve within reason, it will be accomplished.

Language and other cultural barriers may have existed but given the same opportunities and stimulus, each soldier or individual would prevail. Relatively speaking we can all learn and retain, and process information. Some of us may be better at it than others.

It is not a matter of who is or who was the most intelligent. It was a matter of who was provided the necessary tools and stimulants to achieve a desired goal.

Is Everyone Created Equal?

I do not believe that everyone is created equal. The closest we may get to it legally at this point in time is by having identical twins. We all may have more or less the same ingredients that make us all human beings, but the amount that each individual has will differ in varying stages and degrees.

I cannot grow to become a 7' tall and weigh 400 pounds naturally due to my genetical makeup. I cannot read the dictionary and remember the meaning of every word that I have just read. I simply do not have what it takes naturally.

If in fact these were a set standards or goal that were a good one to obtain, I could eat as much food as possible in order to grow and put on weight, I would read, the dictionary over and over until I could remember and recite every meaning for every word. Naturally due to my genetic limitations, my body frame could not sustain 400 lbs. of body weight, I could not grow to be 7' tall, nor could my mind remember or recite an entire dictionary after one reading.

There are people in this world though that may not find this situation simply as challenging as it may appear to many of us and could possibly prove us wrong. We have all known someone at some point in of our lives, or careers, whether it be a classmate, a coworker, a friend or even a stranger that was able to read and recite almost anything without any problems at all, and didn't even need to take notes. We have what I can call slow learners, fast learners, and others that can be classified as gifted. In this same way we have small people, large people, straight, gays, those that are gifted physically, or any combination of the sorts. Our genetical makeup does play a big part in what we do and what we become in life. Though our environment does play a role, I do not believe Michael Jackson, Michael Jordan, Mike Tyson or Richard Simmons would do or become the same thing if they were confined to the exact same environment and set of stimuli as others may want to suggest.

I do not believe Richard Simmons or Michael Jackson would want to become the next heavy weight champion of the world or become one of the greatest basketball players, nor do I think they would be very successful at it. I do not think Mike Tyson or Michael Jordan would want to become one of the greatest music and dance entertainers or fitness trainer who would offer workout routines like

"Dance Your Pants Off," "Disco Sweat," "Blast Off the Pounds," "Sweatin' to the Oldies," "Platinum Sweat," and "Sit Tight," workout routines, nor do I think they would be very successful at it.

It is our ability to realize our unique gifts and talents that each of us was created with and use them in a positive way that will make all the difference.

Technically we can mix and match the genes of a certain breed of things to get a desired result as we do with any other species. However touching on this subject and talking about these issues is much too controversial and morally wrong, as so many of us strongly believe. So even to begin to bring humans into this picture is still too hard to contemplate at this point in time. However even though this may be a very highly controversial subject, we must practice to never shy away from it, or anything that may be controversial, as evident in my writings. It is always best that we address these things in the open before they address us.

We should look to safeguard anything that we deem may be an issue to ensure the safety and longevity of all. We all know or should know by now that man is a very intelligent being, we can do almost anything if we set our minds to it, and like in all areas, sometime profit, money and greed gets the best of us and we may do things that are not in the best interest of everyone. It is very important that we keep this in mind and keep ourselves in check

That being said, everyone has the ability to become great by just being all that they can be. Whatever that God has given us when we were born, we have the ability to use it to its fullest potential. Sadly though many of us do not know what our maximum potential for greatness is because we may never have the intestinal fortitude or the guts to push ourselves to achieve it. In some cases simply not having the opportunity to achieve that greatness is the number one reason, however times have change and the ability to achieve ones personal best is still there for the choosing if one chooses to do so.

As leaders it is very important that we provide the guidance and tools, in an environment that is conducive to doing and becoming the best one can to be a productive citizen. Undoubtedly some will not be capable due to their physical or biological handicaps. However with everything else being equal, the desired output will be achieved, and the products that are achieved will be similar in nature because we are all humans.

As with the young soldier, the better the experience in the early years allowed for an easier assimilation and accomplishment of the various tasks and challenges that they were faced with. New tasks that did not require any prior experience would get similar results all of the time and the standards would be met. It is important that we set high, realistic, and achievable standards and goals for all to follow and hold them accountable for their actions, to include any deviation or breach of those standards if they are within the realm of what we want to accomplish.

The bottom line here is discipline. It is the backbone of the military and it should be the backbone in all that we do. Once we all realize it and carry it over into our civilian lives we can really begin to make things happen. It is one of the most important ingredients required to make a change. It is why I would recommend that everyone, especially the male gender, should serve at least two years in the military or take military courses while in college if they have the chance. Not just for the benefit that they will get from it but for the opportunity to serve his and her country. I think we can all use some military discipline. This is what has made this country so great.

As a soldier we take our jobs very seriously. We believe in our institutions and we strive to be professionals in our fields. We are proud to serve our country and we will continue to serve our country faithfully in times of crisis. As a former member of the 3rd Infantry Division, formerly known as the 24th Infantry Division, I was one of the firsts to go into Iraq. My first tour of duty with the division was as a 2nd Lieutenant in Dessert Storm. The same month that I signed into the division was the same month that we prepared to deploy because the Iraqis had already invaded Kuwait. I deployed with my unit to the Kingdom Saudi Arabia where we sat and waited for the Iraqis to back out from their positions.

After spending many months in the desert waiting it became obvious that the Iraqis were not going to back out. When we finally received the word that we had to go to war to repel the Iraqis, we simply rejoiced because most of us could not wait to simply do our jobs. It was what we prepared for, and knowing that when our jobs were done we could then go back home and see our families. As soldiers what we do is simply the job that we are trained to do nothing else.

As a veteran of Operation Dessert Storm and Iraqi freedom, my efforts to assist my country in its time of crisis were very rewarding. Doing my job was a pleasure from the beginning to the end. The opportunity to have deployed early to the Middle East prior to and in preparation for the wars have given me the opportunity to see how things really were before the fight began and how it is now during the post war occupation. Anyone who has been there as I have before the war will see that things have certainly changed for the better for the Iraqi people. No one can better testify to the appreciation for the job that we do there than our soldiers and the good people of Iraq. Many of our soldiers have been there and have bore the burden of having to compromise those things that many of us take for granted and is willing to do so over and over if called upon so that the rest of us will not have to. That is what good soldiers do. I would also like to take a moment to thank our closest allies like Great Britain and others that have also stood in the trenches and fought alongside the U.S.

We must always remember that we are a super power and we would not have gotten here if it we were not for these soldiers and our leaders who are proactive in ensuring and protecting our freedom. With great power comes great responsibility, we should and cannot turn a blind eye to the potential dangers and atrocities and wrong doings in this world any longer. If we choose to do so and continue to ignore it, it will come back and bite us in the butt when we least expect it as evident in the bombing of the Word Trade Center.

As a soldier and a US citizen my job is to try to ensure that this does not happen again. We are soldiers and this is what soldiers do. We protect and serve to keep our country safe. Yes, it is a dangerous job and we know what the dangers are. We know that some of us may die, we know that all of us will not make it home safe. We were not forced to join, we knowingly and willingly took the oath and signed on the dotted line to defend and protect our country from all enemies foreign and abroad.

Many of us have families at home that we would like to be with and will do anything to keep them safe. We understand and are well aware of the dangers and the sacrifices involved, however if we must go to war we would rather take the fight to our enemies rather than to have them bring it to us again like they have already done on Sep 11th.

I believe we have made all the right moves so far in an effort to try to keep our county and our allies safe. To stand by and do nothing or simply just concentrate and limit ourselves to Afghanistan and finding Bin Laden alone would be fruitless. We have enemies all over the region. Doing what we did, and expanding our thoughts and positions on how we feel about being attacked or this type of retaliation can only be effective if it is done in a big way. I think that possibly if we had done it in a big way long ago then maybe 911 may have never occurred, and we would not be in the situation that we are in now. It was important that we did it in a big way. Doing it this way will clearly send the message to those that do not like us that we will not tolerate the killing of innocent people, change our way of life, or stand by and hope that there is not another attack.

We are simply soldiers, fighting to keep our freedoms and our country safe. It is what we do. What disturbs me most during the 911 attack was that the approximately three thousand innocent civilians were killed and none of them wore the military uniform or had a gun pointed at any of the members or groups that carried out the attack.

It can and may happen again, regardless of whether it may or may not be directly linked to Iraq or the fact that we have gone to war, and if it does hopefully we will continue to respond in kind. The only things we know for sure is that our list of enemies are long and that many in that region have had a long history of violence and Anti-US rhetoric and do not think too kindly of the US and its allies. It is and has been a breeding ground for a lot of anti US rhetoric for quite some time and there are lot of people within that region and even in ours that would like to do us harm if they can. We must attempt to show and convince them that yes we do live a different kind life style, yes we are good people too, and no we will not compromise our freedom.

The best thing that we can do over there is remain involved. By maintaining our presence there we can try to educate and better understand each other and possibly change some of the negative perceptions that we have about one another. At the very least our eyes and ears in some form or fashion must be there at all times to ensure the safety of our American people.

The incident on Sept 11 should never have occurred. It has already taken away some of our freedoms and have drastically changed our way of life forever. We must now live in fear when dealing in certain areas that we know are susceptible to terrorism and hope that if there is another incident we are not one of the lucky ones. Another devastating attack could possibly cripple this country and send everything including our economy into a tailspin.

This is not the way we want to live or lives nor should we. We must and will continue to fight it until we win. We must continue let our enemies know that the killing of innocent civilians is not the way to get even or revenge for whatever political strife's or other frustrations they may have against the United States and its people, or their fellow man. If we did nothing, every one of us to include our children and grand children are potential targets. We must continue take the fight to our enemies because if we don't, as I have mentioned earlier, they will bring it to us time and time again. The best defense is always a strong offense.

Many of us had the opportunity to witness the bombing of the world trade center. For me it was just a wake up call to have seen the destruction that just a few bad people can do to so many of the innocent if we let them. I can understand targeting soldiers, but I just can't understand it when it comes down to targeting innocent civilians.

Real soldiers fight soldiers and bad people to protect their country and to protect their innocent regardless of the sacrifices, and we do so with honor.

As a soldier I would like to recite a poem that was sent to me during the holidays by one of my soldiers who is no longer here that actually describes what it is like to be a true soldier. I think we should all be thankful and proud of our county and the job that our soldiers do to keep this country great.

<u>TWAS THE NIGHT BEFORE CHRISTMAS</u>

"TWAS THE NIGHT BEFORE CHRISTMAS,
HE LIVED ALL ALONE,
IN A ONE BEDROOM HOUSE MADE OF
PLASTER AND STONE.

I HAD COME DOWN THE CHIMNEY
WITH PRESENTS TO GIVE,
AND TO SEE JUST WHO
IN THIS HOME DID LIVE.

I LOOKED ALL ABOUT,
A STRANGE SIGHT I DID SEE,
NO TINSEL, NO PRESENTS,
NOT EVEN A TREE.

NO STOCKING BY MANTLE,
JUST BOOTS FILLED WITH SAND,
ON THE WALL HUNG PICTURES
OF FAR DISTANT LANDS.

WITH MEDALS AND BADGES,
AWARDS OF ALL KINDS,
A SOBER THOUGHT
CAME THROUGH MY MIND.

FOR THIS HOUSE WAS DIFFERENT,
IT WAS DARK AND DREARY,
I FOUND THE HOME OF A SOLDIER,
ONCE I COULD SEE CLEARLY.

THE SOLDIER LAY SLEEPING,
SILENT, ALONE,
CURLED UP ON THE FLOOR
IN THIS ONE BEDROOM HOME.

THE FACE WAS SO GENTLE,
THE ROOM IN SUCH DISORDER,
NOT HOW I PICTURED
A UNITED STATES SOLDIER.

WAS THIS THE HERO
OF WHOM I'D JUST READ?
CURLED UP ON A PONCHO,
THE FLOOR FOR A! BED?

I REALIZED THE FAMILIES
THAT I SAW THIS NIGHT,
OWED THEIR LIVES TO THESE SOLDIERS
WHO WERE WILLING TO FIGHT.

SOON ROUND THE WORLD,
THE CHILDREN WOULD PLAY,
AND GROWNUPS WOULD CELEBRATE
A BRIGHT CHRISTMAS DAY.

THEY ALL ENJOYED FREEDOM
EACH MONTH OF THE YEAR,
BECAUSE OF THE SOLDIERS,
LIKE THE ONE LYING HERE.

I COULDN'T HELP WONDER
HOW MANY LAY ALONE,
ON A COLD CHRISTMAS EVE
IN A LAND FAR FROM HOME.

THE VERY THOUGHT
BROUGHT A TEAR TO MY EYE,

I DROPPED TO MY KNEES
AND STARTED TO CRY.
THE SOLDIER AWAKENED
AND I HEARD A ROUGH VOICE,
"SANTA DON'T CRY,
THIS LIFE IS MY CHOICE;

I FIGHT FOR FREEDOM,
I DON'T ASK FOR MORE,
MY LIFE IS MY GOD,
MY COUNTRY, MY CORPS."

THE SOLDIER ROLLED OVER
AND DRIFTED TO SLEEP,
I COULDN'T CONTROL IT,
I CONTINUED TO WEEP.

I KEPT WATCH FOR HOURS,
SO SILENT AND STILL
AND WE BOTH SHIVERED
FROM THE COLD NIGHT'S CH! ILL.

I DIDN'T WANT TO LEAVE
ON THAT COLD, DARK, NIGHT,
THIS GUARDIAN OF HONOR
SO WILLING TO FIGHT.

THEN THE SOLDIER ROLLED OVER,
WITH A VOICE SOFT AND PURE,
WHISPERED, "CARRY ON SANTA,
IT'S CHRISTMAS DAY, ALL IS SECURE."

ONE LOOK AT MY WATCH,
AND I KNEW HE WAS RIGHT.
"MERRY CHRISTMAS MY FRIEND,
AND TO ALL A GOOD NIGHT."

How We Can Help Our Soldiers

We have one of the best Military in the world that prides itself on doing a good job for our county and keeping its citizen safe. There are many young and impressionable soldiers that prides themselves on doing a good job for their country. To say or insinuate that we are fighting a losing battle and are losing lives for illegitimate reasons is simply not the right time or the things that we like to hear while we are still in combat.

What we should be doing is trying to find out if there is anything more that we can do or should be doing to make our soldiers lives more bearable and rewarding and if there is, it is what we should be doing. We must continue to support our troops at all cost. If we must continue to fight, and we want to help our soldiers then we must ensure that our soldiers are given all the necessary tools and equipment that is necessary to help keep them alive. If there is anything we can still do today other than pull out, in order to help keep our soldiers from becoming casualties from things that may have been preventable like roadside bombs that we hear about almost daily, it is what we must do.

The only thing I would ask is that we continue to support our troops and provide them with whatever supplies they need to keep them alive and do their jobs effectively. Many of the dirty tactics that the enemy has resorted to calls for heavy anti armor vehicles and equipment. There should be no reason why we cannot accommodate our fellow soldiers in this area. I know we have the expertise, the technology and the finance in order to do so if we don't already have the equipment. Let us all try to place the lives of our soldiers ahead of the cost and all the other political issues and road barriers that it would take to make this a reality. After all, if it were not for these brave great young men and women who have fought and died for this great country we would probably be worrying about more important things rather than simply the cost to support our troops.

We are very quick to spend a billion dollars here and a trillion dollars there. For starters, lets decide to spend just a billion dollars on getting our troops better anti-mine and anti armor personnel vehicles and equipment that are not susceptible to many of the road side bombs that arc killing so many of or soldiers that possibly could have been prevented.

There are and will always be people who disagrees and wish that we were out of Iraq for political and economic reasons. However they do not represent the majority of true patriots of the US or the law-abiding citizens of Iraq.

Regardless of what we may see or hear, there are an overwhelming number of law abiding citizens in Iraq that welcomes the United States with open arms but are still too scared to show or say it for fear of being killed.

The Iraqi people in time will eventually take over and run it's own affairs. I believe in time the Iraqis civilians and others in the region that are becoming victims and casualties for no reason at all will rise up and say enough is enough and begin to take control, however it will have to take many more casualties. We must be willing to guarantee them some assurance that we will always be there, in order to support and protect them from the reoccurrence of corruption, reprisals, or possibly another dictator.

It is very easy for someone to lose faith when his or her life is at stake. When and if the faith is lost in their new government the next dictator will be there waiting in the balance and not only just the lives of many of the Iraqis will be at stake once more but also the rest of the free world. We are in too deep now to pull back. To pull out before the job is done should not be an option. Our comrades in arms that are no longer here did not, and should not have died in vain.

We all feel for every soldier and their families who have given their lives for their county. I can sympathize with Cindy Sheehan and the likes, on how she feels about the loss of her son. However, we must not continue to rally and have these anti-war protestors make a circus out of the war while our troops are still fighting. When we do this, all we may be doing is causing more American casualties by inciting the opposition. We are giving them a sense that we are not united and their intended goal is near. We must all stand united. United we will stand, divided we will fall.

The Iraqis deserves to be free as we are. If it were not for this country, its policies and what it stood for, many of us that are currently protesting against the war would probably not be here today, or have had the opportunity to protest freely against anything, for that matter, if it wasn't for similar actions that our government has taken in the past to allow us this freedom.

We have accomplished plenty of good over in the region thus far. Lets not forget all the other good things that we have already accomplished in Afghanistan. We will continue to complete our mission of liberating and supporting the Iraqi people so that they may be able to stand on their own.

There is plenty of good going on behind the scenes that most of us would not know unless we seek this information. Most of us are just simply not interested or really don't care. Many still believe that we are not making any progress and would rather see our troops come home which is understandable if this were the case, but it is not. We are making progress, slowly but surely.

Below are some of the things most of us may not know or care even about, however here are some of the pre war and post war information that may be of interest to some:

Did you know that 47 countries have re-established their embassies in Iraq?

Did you know that the Iraqi government employs 1.2 million Iraqi people?

Did you know that 3100 schools have been renovated, 364 schools are under rehabilitation, 263 schools are now under construction and 38 new schools have been built in Iraq?

Did you know that Iraq's higher educational structure consists of 20 universities, 46 institutes or colleges and 4 research centers?

Did you know that 25 Iraq students departed for the United States in January 2004 for the re-established Fulbright program?

Did you know that the Iraqi Navy is operational? They have five 100-foot patrol craft, 34 smaller vessels and a naval infantry regiment.

Did you know that Iraq's Air Force consists of three operation squadrons, 9 reconnaissance and 3 US C-130 transport aircraft which operate day and night, and will soon add 16 UH-1 helicopters and 4 bell jet rangers?

Did you know that Iraq has a counter-terrorist unit and a Commando Battalion?

Did you know that the Iraqi Police Service has over 55,000 fully trained and equipped police officers?

Did you know that there are 5 Police Academies in Iraq that produce over 3500 new officers each 8 weeks?

Did you know there are more than 1100 building projects going on in Iraq? They include 364 schools, 67 public clinics, 15 hospitals, 83 railroad stations, 22 oil facilities, 93 water facilities and 69 electrical facilities.

Did you know that 96% of Iraqi children under the age of 5 have received the first 2 series of polio vaccinations?

Did you know that 4.3 million Iraqi children were enrolled in primary school by mid October?

Did you know that there are 1,192,000 cell phone subscribers in Iraq and phone use has gone up 158%?

Did you know that Iraq has an independent media that consist of 75 radio stations, 180 newspapers and 10 television stations?

Did you know that the Baghdad Stock Exchange opened in June of 2004?

Of course we did not know this, but if we did would it matter? Probably not for many of us, but it does matter to the Iraqis.

This data will change as we move forward in time and so will the mind and soul of the Iraqi people.

These statistics and facts are verifiable on the Department of Defense web site.

Past and Present Political Leaders and Our Decision to Go To War

Everyone seems to want to criticize our president for not having probable cause to go into Iraq. The president did the right thing. I cannot imagine another president that would not do the same for his country. The thought of not doing anything, especially after what happened on 911 is unimaginable. To have to wait for permission to defend our country against those that we thought might have had something to do with the attack and are capable of having weapons of mass destruction is ridiculous. This attack consisted of only four airplanes, less than two dozen people and took the lives of 3000 innocent people. Let's not wait for them to get five airplanes.

Just the thought of the possibility of Iraq having weapons of mass destruction should not have even been one of the main underlying factors for our invasion. We should have invaded Iraq simply because it was the right thing to do in order to save not just the lives of the Iraqi people but ours and our allies as well. No one has a crystal ball but I believe if we had not gotten involved when we did I dont believe our future, or our allies in the region nor that of the Iraqis would be looking as bright as they are today.

The fact that we had clear evidence that Iraq was being run by a brutal dictator, not playing by the rules of the United Nations, finding numerous mass graves, had already used biological agents on its people and was a threat to international peace should have been enough. To wait until we are sure that a country that does not like us that has an unstable dictator, and has weapons of mass destruction before we go in makes little sense at all if we care anything about our county, our people and our soldiers.

I commend our president for taking a stand on Iraq. I do not believe any other of the candidates that have ran against our president might have had the intestinal fortitude to do the same even though many of them were great leaders. General Wesley Clark was one that I thought could possibly give George Bush Jr. a run for his money. General Wesley Clark is a good man that I though could have competed with the president and not just because he is an ex-military man, but simply because I thought he believed in doing the right thing. The only issue or question that I would have had for Mr. Wesley Clark is why would he be so willing to move into Bosnia when he would not do the same for Iraq?

Both countries have had their leaders commit mass atrocities on its people. Iraq on the other hand not only committed mass atrocities, but clearly presented itself as a more dangerous threat to its people, the stability of the Middle East, the United States and its allies.

John Kerry, John Edwards and others were also good candidates, but for the era that we are in today calls for a more aggressive pro military leader that is willing to take on the international threats that we are facing today.

I believe our current administration is perfectly suited to do this job. All the right avenues are being looked at; two of which I strongly believe are very important which will make a significant difference in our future. One is to continue to work to stabilize the new Iraqi regime, and most importantly we must continue to take an active role in trying to maintain peace between the Palestinian and the Israelis which for a long time have had long standing differences.

Simply by ignoring or not working hard enough on these issues would be a bad choice. If in fact there are tensions in these regions and we choose simply to ignore them, it will do noting but continue to brew. At some point this brew may have a tendency to spill over and if we are in the kill range we may all be susceptible in some way, fashion or form to collateral damages that can occurs when this brew spills over.

Our relationship with our allies continues to be an important one. It appears that there will always be a disgruntled sect or group out there somewhere looking to lash out at its enemies, and their enemy's allies. They may see us and other powerful countries as someone who can help them in their plight but are unsympathetic or not concerned with them or their struggles and more favorable in a relationships with their enemies. They may get the feeling that the cards are stacked against them and may lash out in ways that are unacceptable.

Our fight against terrorism thus far has been successful. I cannot think of anyone in our entire administration that was more willing and able to take on the terrorist than our current president. Not just for the heartfelt sorrow that he so openly displayed for the victims of 911, but also for the county he truly loves.

I have grown to learn that regardless of whatever decision one make there will be plenty of criticism to go around, especially if the decision did not turn out as we expected. In this "New World" of politics, no one is immune to prosecution, accusation or slander anymore in or government. There is no set loyalty when it comes to concealing and protecting those for doing what's right or wrong within either political party any more, which is a good thing. As I have alluded to earlier, self-cleansing within government and both political parties will continue to define itself into something that we all can be proud of. This is definitely a positive for everyone so lets continue to let the cards fall where they may.

Many of these positive changes have come under or current president George W. Bush and his administration and will continue as long as we keep him and his administration at the wheel. What I like about our president is that he has always been straightforward and forth coming with the people for whatever decisions or actions he has made, and he is not afraid to let you know if he does not like you. If there was a decision to be made by him or any of his cabinet members and it happened to be the wrong, he would be quick to take the blame and claim responsibility and tell us why he has made the decision. In most cases there is very few decisions that our president can or will make without the advice of his cabinet members, and if he did not think it was right, or right for this country, he would not have made it.

Despite all the rhetoric, Iraq has been liberated. It now has the potential to be anything and everything that it would have never had opportunity to be or do in the past and so does its people. The entire region now has the potential to benefit from their new government. There are no doubts in my mind that they will prosper as a result of this war. They will, but it will take some time. As they slowly embrace a new government that is more in line with the spirit of western democracy the possibilities for the people of Iraq will get better.

We may have won the fight, however we have not yet won the war. We still have plenty of work to do. Internationally the world is now a safer place as a direct result of the war, however domestically speaking; it is still too much of a dangerous place. With the support of everyone, we can, we must, and we will win this war no matter how long it takes. We must never forget the sacrifices of our soldiers or those that have lost their lives in the tragedy of September 11th 2001.

How soon we tend to forget some of our major tragedies. I will always remember this little poem from a former marine that I have had the opportunity to work with side by side. It will always seem to ring true as we triumph from one major crisis to another, which went like this:

"God and ammo we adore, in times of crisis not before, Problem solved crisis righted, Gods forgotten, ammo slighted".

Sad but true.

Politics and Changes

Over the years my political views have changed. I believe in time both the democratic and political parties will eventually merge into one. The Democratic Party had already done its Job. Back in the fifties, sixties, seventies and even the early eighties, there were very few if any minority that could have been part of the Republican Party unless they were just simply out of touch with reality.

The Job of growing the government and enacting legislation to ensure equal rights and ban discrimination was passed. Dr Martin Luther King and his dream did not die in vain. To bring us to where we are now required strong leadership on both ends. Dr Martin Luther King and his closest supporters could not have done it alone. The burden also fell on the backs of blacks and whites alike in and outside of the government.

Understandingly there will always be some within the Democratic Party that may find it too difficult to let go, or simply do not have a choice but to stick to their party lines because of its history. Their feelings and history may be tied to some of the heavy losses that have occurred during those trouble times in the past where many were willing to put their careers and lives on the line for what they thought was right. Without them we would not have gotten this far no matter how long or short of a distance we think we may have come. We should never forget that, and should always be thankful for their hard work and sacrifices.

There are bad apples in every administration, however times have changed. People are a lot more educated today than they were back in the 1950's, 60's and 70's. There is a new generation of leaders that have, and are evolving in both parties that are mentally, physically, morally and ethically qualified to hold these positions and continue lead this country in the right direction.

I believe in time both parties will eventually cleanse itself of any injustices within as we have been witnessing over the past couple years. With time justice will prevail as it always has, and both parties will become a party of one. It is now time for both sides to work together and move on.

The Democratic Party has done a good job and has served its purpose. We must move on. It is getting harder and harder to make up for the injustices of the past without creating more inequities. What has been done is done, what was taken away is gone. I don't believe any of us on either side of the fence are old enough to have participated in the injustices in the past and if there are then there should be no statute of limitation to pursue these individuals.

My philosophy is that everyone is an individual and should be viewed and treated as such. What our ancestors have done in the past is not a reflection of what we might do or how we should feel today. We must simply learn from their mistakes and try to make better decisions and move on.

The struggle for equality has long been fought and won politically. We can never stop discrimination. At this point it is not a political action that will change how people feel and think, nor can we totally control what they do. It is the individual's will to do so that will.

The difference in deciding how to act or react with or without any kind of governmental pressure, regulations or political pressure will still fall on the shoulders of the individuals. The fact is that, there are, and there will always be people who will always be looking backwards and operating as such. They will continue to look and find a way out, and in most cases they will find one if they really want to and no amount of pressure can force someone to change his or her feelings if they don't want to. The only thing that government or we can do is make laws, repeal laws, and prosecute if a violation of the law is detected.

The best way to bring on changes is by facing it head-on, and this is where a good strong leader will make the difference. This leader must be within the strongest party and have the committed staff principles on his or her staff or administration that are willing to back him up in order to effect or make positive changes. Our current administration under President George W. Bush Jr. has just that, and is fully qualified to make and encourage those positive changes.

The democratic party can and should continue to serve its purpose by keeping a watchful eye on what is taking place and report discrepancies to the people who will in turn bring it to light in order to effect change. Simply just by placing a democratic candidate in office would not be a good thing. The right changes are being made for the better as we move into the 21st century under our current administration. Under our current administration we have begun to see return to core values as Americans which embraces many of the moral and ethical issues that so many are concerned about.

Under our former administration many of these issues were initially brought to the forefront some would argue for political reasons. Whatever the real reason, it has turned out to be a good thing, which has benefited everyone. It has served as a catalyst for drawing attention and opening the eyes of many Americans. Prompting all American to pay closer attention to who we choose to lead this country. From the president, the members of his or her cabinet, legislative staff members and the likes will now have to face the scrutiny of people.

This type of scrutiny is not limited to the United States government and its legislative branches. It has now filtered over into Corporate America and down to our local governments.

Even corporate corruption is on mend. The fallout of the stock market back in early 2000 involved not only the small investors, but also many of the high rollers. The larger investors who also fell victim and lost lots of money in the meltdown were primarily the ones that generated a call for a closer look into the financial dealings and management of investor's funds. This issue became one of the hottest issues during our previous and present administration.

With the prosecution of Martha Stewart, Sam Waksal of ImClone, Enron, and Former Worldcom Executive Bernie Ebbers, we are well on our way to returning honesty and integrity to the markets. According to the media, the case against Ms. Stewart, the former chairwoman and chief executive of Martha Stewart Living Omnimedia. Ms Stewart received inside information from her friend Samuel Waksal who runs a biotech company that she held shares in. The stock was going to lose value because the drug that was up for approval by the FDA was denied. Ms Stewart was privy to this information through Dr. Waksal and acted on it by selling her stocks before the news was officially out. Dr. Waksal was charged and is serving a seven-year prison term after pleading guilty to several crimes, including securities fraud, most of them related to the sale of ImClone shares he and relatives owned.

Martha Stewart sold approximately 4,000 shares of ImClone Systems worth about $225,000. Though this amount is very little, in comparison to others, it clearly sends the message that no one should be above the law. With the prosecution and verdict of 62 year old Martha Stewart, Dr. Waksal and others, these verdict will continue to send a message that the authorities would protect the integrity of the markets and would not tolerate dishonesty and corruption. By going after the big fish and acting swiftly to bring them to justice will continue to discourage dishonest brokers and officials not engage in this type of conduct.

In a good and bad way, it took loosing millions of small and large investor's dollars to bring the corruption to light. Not only did the small investors get burnt, but many of the large corporations also got caught in the tailspin. This tailspin was able to grab the attention of many of the big players, which made it a lot easier to investigate and go after the kingpins.

This new scrutiny and demand for a tougher more responsible and honest government can only be good, and not just for corporate corruption and our political parties, but good for the entire country and our nation.

From the Military Back to the Street

I will now take you back to my home town of Atlanta Georgia where I returned after completing my tour of duty in the military. I have returned to the street of Atlanta to continue to pursue my fight against crime and injustice as a police officer. In my view, Atlanta is on of the cities I believe that has the greatest opportunity and potential to become the "Model City" that we all want.

It is now one of the most diverse and upcoming cities in the country. There is a mixture of all races and backgrounds and nationalities from all over the nation. It is no longer the stereotypical place that we use to think of when we thought about the Deep South. There may now be just as much northerners and foreigners here as there are southerners.

It is the home and birthplace of some of the greatest leaders in black history. Great leaders like The Reverend Dr Martin Luther king, Maynard Jackson and others. It maintains an impressive historical track record for people from all walks of life but is know particularly for the advancement of colored people, women, and in recent years the gay and lesbian community and others, as I will explain later on.

It is one of the first cities in the south to have fought hard to have broken the racial divide and took it to another level. One of the first cities in the south to have had a African American female Police Chief, an African-American Mayor, and other governmental departments and department heads that are dominated by African Americans. For a long time the city of Atlanta had been governed by a small circle of civil rights sympathizers which helped to bring some positive changes to the city as it related to race relations and giving well needed opportunities such as jobs and other benefits to minorities in the city.

It appeared that everything was fine for quite some time in this respect, however as time went on and the struggle for equality subsided, it became very difficult for any outsider to get in, especially in higher branches or echelons of the government within the city. It was very difficult for an outsider unless you were part of that inner circle. In a sense it was good during those times in order to try and even out the playing fields.

With the death of Maynard Jackson and the loss of many of his predecessors signals the beginning of a new generation as we witness this era slowly passing by the wayside.

Times have changed. We are no longer pulling from inside that circle and are now looking elsewhere to bring in outsiders that can bring positive changes to the city and its numerous departments. We are opening the doors to new leadership, new ideas and new opportunities that will take us into the 21st century.

A new order of checks and balances as it relates to personnel and management are filtering in throughout the system, and helping to provide a more efficient and effective style of leadership and government.

With the selection of a new Mayor, Shirley Franklin, and a new Atlanta Police Chief, Richard Pennington, it is no longer business as usual. They have taken the reigns and have made some drastic and positive changes inside and out. These two key leaders and positions in my opinion are two of the most important positions in the shaping and the reshaping of any city. It is very important that they set the high standards that will take the city to where it wants to be.

My observation of their actions and the issues that these two great leaders have undertaken and tackled so far deserves honorable mention. No one prior to them has had the courage to bring the real issues to the forefront and tackle them head on as they have done.

They have made a lot of the tough decisions by exposing, and addressing many of the long neglected problems areas within the city, and its departments. This involves many of the critical issues as it relates to addressing some of the ethical issues, addressing crime problems, and tackling the cities much needed infrastructure problems and multi-million dollar improvement projects which is currently underway. An improved system of checks and balances throughout the ranks of the city government and its city employees were put in place among other important issues and tasking that are crucial to any city in order to flourish. Though many of their problems were inherited from past administrations, they are able to face them head on in order to get the job done.

With the changing demographics, increase in population, and increase in demand on the infrastructure these must needed changes are critical for the future of Atlanta which warrant the need for this type of dynamic leadership from top to bottom in nearly all the major departments of the city. Exposing problem areas and applying a fair and balanced solution to improve and fix them is what great leaders do. These two leaders have done so, and have done so aggressively.

One of the areas that needed improvement and have significantly improved was the Police Department. I believe the Atlanta Police Department if not now, has the potential of becoming one of the best is the nation. I believe it is among one of the hardest working Police Department in the Nation. Statistically speaking in comparison to the size of the department and the population that it serves, the Atlanta Police Department probably works harder and locks up more people on a daily basis than any other police department in the country. Not only because of these two key leadership positions at the top that works great together when it comes to handling crime and are both strong advocates for enforcing the laws, but simply the fact that Atlanta is rapidly becoming one of the biggest and busiest cities in the south and its citizens are becoming less tolerant of those that break our laws.

If there was one department in this nation that I think honestly need and deserved an increase in officers salary for the amount of work that is generated, it would be this one thumbs down. Understandingly many of the officers like myself do this job simply for benefit we get from helping others, as like some school teachers, firemen and others in similar professions. If money were the sole motivating factor for us doing our jobs, then many of us would not be here and quite frankly, would be better off elsewhere for the sake of the public and ourselves.

However comparatively speaking, in terms of the importance that these professions are or can be in the development and effects that it has on people and their communities, in my opinion is still grossly underpaid. We should all take a look at how we can better serve these workers for their selfless service in the job that they do which deserves the utmost respect.

Low paying jobs are usually systemic throughout most city governments. However it appears that city of Atlanta has remained unusually stagnant for quite some time. I believe there are several reasons for it that are more or less just a little different than other cities. Historically workers in the city were usually unskilled and were willing to work for low pay. Many had no real marketable skills outside of the city, and many became complacent and content with the mere fact of just having a job and receiving a paycheck regularly. As long as enough money was made in order to make ends meet and the cost of living remains low everyone could get by. Just getting by back then was the norm.

Over the years we have seen a substantial increase in the population in the city. Individual wants and needs have also changed with the changes in demographics. This increase has driven up the cost of living and competition for the natives of Atlanta. Competition has entered the market, which is demanding more and more skilled workers. The competitive natures for many of the natives of Atlanta were not being exercised, nor were there a good enough reason to. However times have changed and those that were not, and are not involved with these changes will, and are finding themselves further and further behind the power curve where the divide between the rich and poor will continue to widen.

Population and competition is increasing at a much faster pace. Not only is it taking a toll on the city workers, and the native Atlantans, but the increase in the population is also taking a toll on the city's infrastructure. It appears that the increase in population will continue outpace whatever improvements are being made for the future and by time these projects are completed it may be time again for another overhaul. However I am pretty confident that with the current leadership and their current administration in place, the right things are being accomplished to overcome these needs and challenges in the future.

Everyone knows we cannot stop progress. The only other suitable alternative is finding more ways to build and improve our people, our city government, and its infrastructures so that we are smart enough, large enough and strong enough to sustain the large migration of people who are coming to Atlanta to make it their home.

Though we are only talking about the city of Atlanta, I am pretty sure there are other cities out there that will experience more or less some of these similar effects.

Yes, competition is in full effect. It is also important that we also keep an eye on the bigger picture. It is not only local competition that is going on that we should be concerned about, there is global and international competition as well, in and out of our county for jobs and other things that we once took for granted. We must not limit ourselves as we move forward. Whatever we can do to better prepare ourselves and not lose our edge, if in fact we do have and edge, it is what we must do.

Changes in Our Communities and My Thoughts on the Gay and Lesbian Community

Another large segment of people that have grown tremendously in Atlanta is the gay and lesbian community. Over the years Atlanta has seen the growth of a very large and open gay and lesbian community, not typical for a small southern city. The tolerance level for a southern city is normally very low towards these types of lifestyles but again, this in another example of how the south has changed. Many have migrated to the city in the more affluent areas of the city.

My thoughts on gays are that they are no different than any of us that are heterosexual other than the biological factors at it relates to their genetics makeup. They should be able to enjoy all the same rights, benefits and freedom that we all share as an Americans. There are many different arguments, theories etc. as to why some people are gay and why others are not. I am no expert on this subject but I don't think we need to be an expert on many of the things that many of us find so difficult to understand.

My take on this issue is that I believe that we are all what we are when we are born. It is our biological makeup that I have referred to on so many occasions that determines our fate when it relates to this subject and many others that I have already cited in this book. Being gay have nothing to do with his or her choosing. By the time we are born it is too late to decide on whether we will be gay or not, we can only choose the type of lifestyle we prefer to live. If given a choice between being straight or gay, I believe most if not all would choose to be straight.

I do not believe we can learn to be gay, we can only learn gay behaviors and perform homosexual acts, but that in itself does not make us gay. Some of us may believe it is an illness that may be cured through therapy. In my view there is noting that we can do to make someone straight or gay unless we can somehow change the biological makeup, which has nearly everything to do with their genes, hormones etc, that are within each individual. These factors are unique to the individual as DNA is to each person.

I will give you an example of what I am talking about and try to make it very simple for all to understand. For example; lets take a scale from 1 to 10, number 1 being as feminine as we can get, which consist of all the biological factors that makes us feminine, and 10 being as macho as we can get which consist of all the biological factors that makes us macho. Each of us falls within one of those ranges. If we are closer to the 10 range we are more male than we are female. If we are closer to the 1 range we are more female than we are male. If we are at the 5, then we can go either way, which is where true bisexuals would fall on this scale. Our minds are simply in control of our bodies. What we do, what we feel, and who we are, are simply under its control. Even though our bodies may look contradicting, it cannot feel a certain way nor do certain things unless our brain tells it to. It is the brain that controls the body, not the body that controls the brain. This is simply my theory, others as you will see below, also has some merits, however in time I think many of us will come around to see it the way that I have just explained.

Dean Hamer, an American researcher published research in 1933 that seemed to prove that homosexual orientation could be genetically transmitted to men on the x chromosome, which they get from their mothers. However when this study was duplicated it did not produce the same results. A follow-up study, which Hamer collaborated on also, failed to reinforce his earlier results.

Most recently research published in April 1999 by George Rice and George Ebers of the University of Western Ontario has cast doubt on Hamer's theory. Rice and Ebers' research also tested the same region of the x chromosome in a larger sample of gay men, but failed to find the same 'marker' that Hamer's research had produced. Claims that the part of the brain known as the hypothalamus is influential in determining sexual orientation have yet to be substantiated. At the moment we still do not have enough evidence, but in time I believe that it will be proven.

Psychosocial explanations also offer a variety of factors that could contribute to the development of a person's homosexuality. For example, a female dominated upbringing in a gay man's past, with an absence of a male role model. Others stress adherence or deviance from conformity to gender roles, and individual psychological makeup. While none of these factors alone completely answers the question 'what causes homosexuality?' they rule out some things. For example, lesbian and gay young people are not 'failed' heterosexuals. Also, homosexual partners are generally of the same age proving wrong the assumptions that young people are 'turned gay' by older people.

What is clear is that people's behavior is influenced by their family environment, their experiences and their sense of themselves. Beliefs about sex are initially shaped by family values. Later on these beliefs may be shaped by pleasant and unpleasant experiences of sex and also shape their choice of activities and partners. Throughout their life a person's sense of who and what they are has a strong impact on their sexual development and experience.

Some people believe homosexuality is an illness and believe it can and should be cured. Many of these cures revolve around psychological therapies, which tries to change a homosexual sexuality to heterosexual. Although there is little scientific data to evaluate, what is available seems to indicate that this therapy is ineffective. American Psychological Association (APA), the world's largest association of psychologists has stated that:

> "Homosexuality is not a mental disorder and the APA opposes all portrayals of lesbian, gay and bisexual people as mentally ill and in need of treatment due to their sexual orientation."

Someone who is gay and is afraid to express him or herself will only continue to suppress those feeling. He or she will continue to be in denial, they will continue to lie to themselves and their communities and be forever unfulfilled. Passing laws or legislation will only force more suppression and deny them of the individual rights they deserve that are afforded to everyone under the U.S. Constitution regardless of sex or gender.

As the truth continues to come out like it always will and everyone begins to finally realize and accept the fact that we really are what we are, we will become more accepting of the gay and lesbian lifestyle. We will continue to see more shows like Queer Eye for the Straight Guy, more people like Ellen DeGeneres, and more start up Broadcast Companies like Triangle Multimedia Company and Q Television Networks coming out of the woodwork in this highly lucrative market sector that is still virtually untapped.

The Future of America and Our Similarities

We are all more alike than we are different. We all generally have the same goals and want the same things in life for our families and ourselves regardless of race or ethnicity. Together we can continue build strong communities by working with our government and government officials to provide a safer and better environment for the citizens of our country and our nation.

America will do just fine as we move into the 21st century. As we move into the 21st century, more emphasis is being place on censorship in order to ban inappropriate materials, new emphasis on values, ethical and moral standards are taking hold once more.

With the problems of past administration, Americans are now keeping a more watchful eye on everything and everyone. We are beginning to realize the fact that eventually no one will, or should be immune from scrutiny or prosecution, and should be held accountable for their actions, and even those of others if they are responsible. These issues that are important to the American people were always there, however it did not appear as if they were being addressed properly. Whether they were brought to the forefront for political reason or not, the American people quickly latched on and have now taken it to another level.

Conclusion

I have taken you on a short journey of events from the streets of New York and back to the streets of Atlanta Georgia. In conclusion there is no one country or no one person that is perfect. We can only try and do the best that we can do. America and its people have been there and are doing just that despite all of the other distractions in the world or what others may think. We still manage to hold our own. We must continue to be vigilant in protecting our freedoms where and whenever it is infringe upon and not loose our edge.

America is the land of the free and the home of the brave. There is no other country like it in the world. Justice in due time will always prevails. We must continue to lead as one of the greatest leaders of the free world and hopefully as time passes us by, others will follow, preferably by choice when given the opportunity.

Opportunity is the key. As Martin Luther King once said, "let freedom ring, let freedom ring". Freedom gives us the opportunity. If the ringer does not exist or the ringer becomes ineffective, we must ensure that it is repaired or replaced with one that will.

We were all born free as god intended us to be. What we choose to do within reason as responsible individuals as long as it does not negatively affect others and society should be respected.

We must continue to ensure that the opportunity is there, and that the sound of freedom will continue to resonate from mountainside to mountainside and from shore to shore to keep this county and our nation great.

Americans are decent, loving and compassionate peace loving people. We can also become as fearsome and dangerous, as we are great and generous in our compassion.

War has come to America and "we will bear the burden, pay any price, oppose any foe" to defend our democracy and our liberty. Make no mistake about it.

We need to remember that American's come in all colors, accents, and faiths, etc. We are all in this together, and together we will prevail against all odds, to include terrorists and bad people in and outside of our country.

God grants liberty only to those who love it and are always ready to guard and defend it, and that we will.

God Bless America!